The Tolkien Scrapbook

The Tolkien Scrapbook

Edited by Alida Becker

Illustrations by Michael Green

Color Illustrations by Tim Kirk

Publishers · GROSSET & DUNLAP · New York
A FILMWAYS COMPANY

9-20-80
C. 27

Copyright © 1978 by Running Press
All rights reserved
Published simultaneously in Canada
Library of Congress catalog card number: 78-65276
ISBN 0-448-16455-8
1978 printing
Printed in the United States of America

Contents

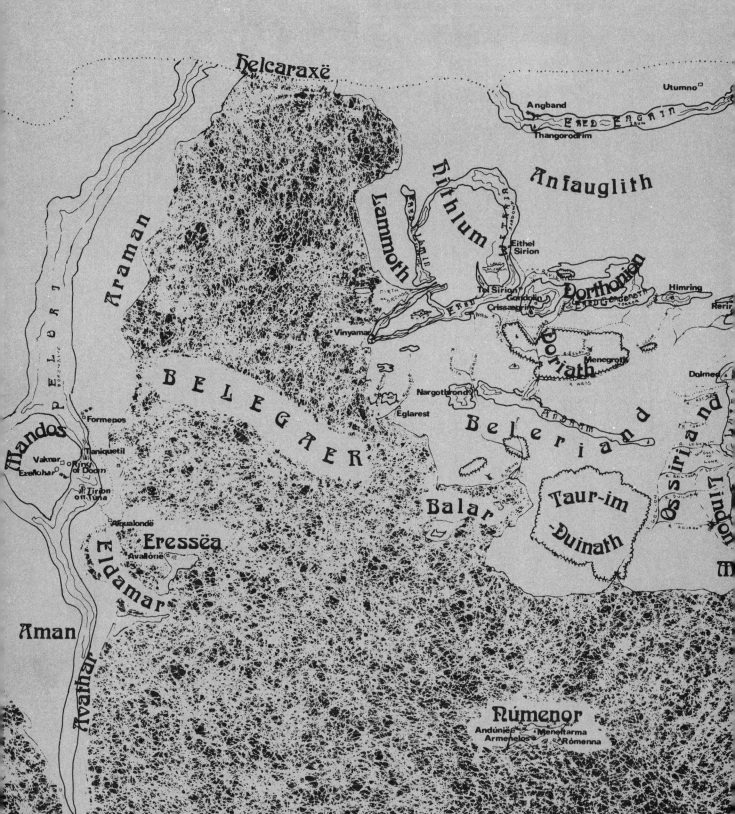

Helcaraxë

Utumno

Angband

ERED ENGRIN

Thangorodrim

Anfauglith

Araman

Lammoth

Hithlum

Eithel
Sirion

Dorthonion

Himring

Tol Sirion

Gondolin

Rerir

Crissaegrim

Vinyamar

Doriath

Dolmed

PELORI

Menegroth

BELEGAER

Nargothrond

Beleriand

Ossiriand

Formenos

Eglarest

Mandos

Valmar

Ring
of Doom

Taniquetil

Balar

Taur-im
-Duinath

Lindon

Ezellohar

Tirion
on Tuna

Aman

Alqualondë

Eressëa

Eldamar

Avallónë

Avathar

Númenor

Andúnië

Meneltarma

Armenelos

Rómenna

EKKAIA

Part I.
Tolkien and Middle-earth

N
W ← → E
S

NORTHERN WASTE

ERED MITHRIN

Arnor

Fornost

Rivendell

Mirkwood

Erebor

IRON HILLS

Moria

Dol Guldur

Rhûn

SEA OF RHÛN

Eriador

Middle-earth

Fangorn

Isengard

Aglarond

Rohan

Argonath

BROWN LANDS

Ered Nimrais

Erech

Gondor

Minas Tirith

Anduin Osgiliath

Ered Lithui

Barad-dûr

Mt Doom

Mordor

Dol Amroth

Pelargir

SEA OF NÚRNEN

Belfalas

Núrn

Umbar

Harad

Cuiviénen

(Illuin)

SEA OF HELCAR

Orocarni

Hildórien

Map of Arda

- 2 trees-Telperion, Laurelin
  3 Silmarils
- White trees
- 7 Palantíri
- Nauglamír
- Felagund's ring
- 3 Elven Rings
- Ruling Ring
- Narsil

(Ormal)

100 200 300 400

J. R. R. Tolkien: A Short Biography

by Joan McClusky

John Ronald Reuel Tolkien. John and Ronald are ordinary enough as names go. Reuel, a family name and his father's middle name, means "friend of God" in Hebrew. Tolkien gave it to each of his four children, and they in turn gave it to their children. It's one sign of the kind of man Tolkien was. In the thirties, he was a member of an Oxford group known as the Inklings whose members were described as "avowedly Christian, conservative, and romantic (in that order)." It's a good idea to keep those things in mind. J.R.R. Tolkien had a wide variety of interests, and his life followed a rather crooked path. But the name "Reuel" seems to have meant something, for anything that might have turned him the "wrong" way seems to have turned out right in the end.

Tolkien was born in Bloemfontein, in what is now South Africa, in 1892. His parents, Arthur and Mabel, were English immigrants who met and married in Africa. Both were bright, ambitious people, solid citizens who also had a spirit of adventure that would be passed on to their son.

Arthur Tolkien was the eldest of a large family. In Victorian England, it was not unusual for the eldest to stay at home and help out until the youngest had left the nest. Arthur did exactly that, working as a clerk in Birmingham until he was free of family demands. At that point, he packed his bags and was off—to manage a new English bank in Bloemfontein, the frontier town that was the capital of the Orange Free State. Arthur was fairly old when he married—again, he followed the conservative approach and waited until he could support a wife in the proper manner. His bride, Mabel Suffield, was a highly religious woman, literate and well bred, who had been brought up in a town about twenty miles from Birmingham. She and her two sisters had gone to Africa to become missionaries.

When Tolkien was born, Bloemfontein was still a pioneer town, an oasis in the desert climate of the Orange Free State; it was not until the year Tolkien was born that railway service to Cape Town was introduced. Tolkien, his younger brother, Hilary, and Arthur and Mabel were four of the roughly 2,000 Europeans in a town with a population of 25,000. They lived in one of the large, European homes in the center of town, and were well tended by the black servants who lived on Bloemfontein's outskirts.

How the natives felt about the European intruders is not well known; although the word "apartheid" had not yet been coined, the domination of the whites over the blacks was very much a part of life. One native houseboy named Isaac was very proud of his position, and would later name his son Isaac Mister Tolkien Victor (the Victor for Victoria, the Queen). However, fondness for his employers and the English monarch did not stop at names. One day, Isaac decided to show off the three-year-old Tolkien to his family. The trip lasted only a few days, but since neither Mabel nor Arthur had been informed of Isaac's plans, there was a great uproar. Although Tolkien was never in any danger and remembered the incident with great amusement in later years, it was one of the major adventures in his young life.

Tolkien was not a hardy child; both he and his brother, Hilary, were small and weak, and the climate of South Africa did not seem to agree with them. Neither did the animal life—Tolkien was stung by a tarantula and detested spiders for the rest of his life. What with the heat, the tarantulas, and Isaac, it's not suprising that, after a great deal of deliberation, Mabel decided to return to England with her two small sons. They would rejoin Arthur when the boys were strong enough to cope with Africa, or when Arthur decided to leave the bank in Bloemfontein and return to England.

Tolkien left Africa with his mother and brother in 1895. Years later, he remembered that he'd been struck by the notion that he would never see his father again. And it was true. Arthur came down with acute peritonitis a few months after his wife and sons left; the illness was apparently the result of his failure to be treated for a mild case of the flu. Perhaps in some way Tolkien blamed himself for his father's death. His mother had left because of the boys' poor health, and if she had been there to look after him, Arthur might well have lived.

Mabel settled with her two sons in Sarehole, a rural town near Birmingham. Tolkien once remarked that Sarehole was "a kind of lost paradise"; it was that same rural England that had existed for centuries and still survived in some places until the First World War. Tolkien remembered that when he arrived at Sarehole, he had a "strange sense of coming home." In later life, the people of

Sarehole would become the hobbits, and the countryside the Shire.

It is no wonder that Tolkien chose such a setting for his stories. The Shire was the rural England he had known and loved as a child. "I loved it with an intensity of love that was a kind of nostalgia reversed," he once said, admitting that "the Shire is very like the kind of world in which I first became aware of things." It must have been difficult for him, though; the world in which he grew up, which he loved deeply, was not really his world. "I took the idea of the hobbits from the village people and children. The hobbits are just what I should like to have been, but never was."

Sarehole was good for Tolkien. He took long walks in the country and grew to know the people and the landscape intimately. "I could draw you a map of every inch," he declared when he was 74. Though they did not have much money, Mabel and Hilary and he were better off than most of the villagers; they lived in genteel poverty rather than with a real sense of deprivation. They were different from the villagers in the way they spoke, and the way they dressed. Tolkien's mother liked her children to dress well, and they wore Little Lord Fauntleroy suits, cartwheel hats, and red satin bows at their collars. "The village children rather despised me," he recalled.

Tolkien was a precocious child—he had invented three or four languages by the age of ten. His mother disapproved of such activities because they took away from the time he should have spent studying; the family did not have much money, and Mabel was determined that her son would have a proper education. She had been a governess before she went to Africa, and after teaching him to read and write, she introduced him to Latin, Greek, mathematics, and novels. Tolkien was a lazy student, but so quick that he seemed to learn whether he wanted to or not.

When Mabel was not teaching her sons, she read them fairy tales; she was a profound romantic, and a nature lover. If one remembers the description of the Inklings—including Tolkien—as Christian, conservative, and romantic, it's not hard to see how much of an influence Mabel had on her sons, especially her eldest.

When Tolkien was about eight, Mabel became a convert to Catholicism. This was something of an act of bravery—Catholicism was still suspect in Birmingham, and Mabel had to rely on the kindness of her Protestant family in order to survive. Nevertheless, Tolkien was enrolled in a school run by the Oratory fathers, a special order founded by John Henry Newman, who had been an Anglican priest before becoming a Catholic. The Oratory was a blend of Anglicanism and Roman Catholicism, and was somewhat, although not entirely, acceptable to most people. While at the school, Tolkien was befriended by Father Francis Xavier Morgan, who became a friend of the family and eventually acted as a surrogate father to both Tolkien and his brother Hilary. Morgan was half Spanish, a bright, gentle man with a sharp intellect.

In 1903, Tolkien sat for and won a scholarship to the King Edward VI School in Birmingham, the best preparatory school in the area. From there, if he did well, he might win a scholarship to a university. King Edward's School had been founded in 1552 by Henry VIII, who named it for his son. It was a good school, not as prestigious as Eton or Harrow, but every year a few of its students managed to win places at Oxford or Cambridge. Mabel would not live to see any of this, however, for she died in 1904, when Tolkien was twelve. It was the second great tragedy to mark his young life.

Mabel apparently had premonitions of her death and made arrangements for the boys should she die before they were grown. She was especially concerned that if they were sent to live with relatives, they might be persuaded to leave the Catholic church. To prevent this, she had to find another way to provide for her sons, so before her death, Mabel asked Father Francis to become their legal guardian. He in turn enrolled the boys in a private orphanage run by the Oratory. Although money was very limited, the two brothers were able to share a private room, and Father Francis would take them for long walks in the countryside on weekends.

The orphanage was built on the outskirts of the grey, industrial city of Birmingham in an area known as "black country" because of the hundreds of smokestacks spewing dark clouds into the sky. It was a far cry from the rural countryside of Sarehole, and although Tolkien enjoyed the city's libraries, museums, and schools, he missed the peace and beauty of the countryside.

To help assuage the pain Tolkien felt at the loss of his mother and the rural world he had loved, he turned back to his imagination. When Father Francis took the brothers on a trip to Wales, Tolkien was struck by the movement and beauty of the language. "Welsh always attracted me more than any other language," said Tolkien years later. After the trip, he began to invent his own languages again.

Tolkien was doing well at school, but not because of any great effort on his part. He himself always admitted that he was "one of the idlest boys" the headmaster ever had. He would be this way throughout life, always succeeding academically, yet forever procrastinating. But Tolkien could be quite energetic about one kind of study—languages. He decided to learn Anglo-Saxon and Welsh on his own. This project might have floundered had a teacher not taken an interest in his efforts after noticing him struggling over Anglo-Saxon literature in the library. George Brewton arranged for private tutorials with the boy, and after Tolkien had mastered the grammar and pronunciation of Anglo-Saxon, Brewton began teaching him Anglo-Saxon literature.

By the time he was sixteen, Tolkien had mastered Latin and Greek and was becoming deeply immersed in Anglo-Saxon literature. As always, his own interests were more absorbing than those dictated by others, but he was so bright that he had few problems in keeping up with his other subjects. He was a good-looking, shy boy who got along well with others. His early frailty had vanished; he was now playing rugby on the school's first team.

That same determination to pursue his own interests also influenced a more romantic relationship. When he fell in love with another orphan, Edith Mary Bratt, Tolkien was only sixteen. She was two years older than he, and not a Catholic, but he was determined to marry her, and eventually he did.

Their early romantic life was not without some troubles, however. Edith was concerned that Tolkien and Hilary never seemed to get enough to eat. She persuaded a maid to help her rig up a trolley system between the kitchen and the boys' bedroom, and every night, a pulley would lower food through their window. When the landlady discovered what was going on, the relationship between Edith and Tolkien was revealed as well. Edith was sent to live with an aunt and uncle, and she and Tolkien were forbidden to see, visit, or write to each other. This ruling held firm until Edith had reached adulthood and Tolkien was at Oxford.

In 1910, Tolkien took a scholarship examination for a place at Exeter College, Cambridge. The King Edward VI School had one "exhibition" place at Exeter, and while Tolkien won the place, he did it just barely, and both he and the college knew he could have done much better on the exam.

Tolkien "went up" to Oxford in the autumn, or Michaelmas, term in 1911. His official title was "A Classical Exhibitioner in Residence at Exeter College." "Exhibitioners" and "scholars" were students who were attending Oxford solely because of their academic ability; their fees were paid by scholarship. A scholar was usually considered more of a gentleman simply because those awards often went to students from upper-middle-class schools. A "commoner," was someone who paid his own fees, and so was usually from the upper classes. Scholars and exhibitioners were thought to be brighter and more academically oriented than commoners, and the black academic gowns they were required to wear outside their rooms varied slightly. However, they all shared the same classes, tutors, and living quarters, and their academic degrees were the same.

As a classical exhibitioner at Exeter College, Tolkien had won the place offered by the college for scholarship graduates of King Edward's School; he had studied classics there and would continue to do so at Oxford. Tolkien would concentrate on the language, literature, philosophy, and history of Greece and Rome, with optional courses in modern subjects.

The college itself was primarily a place of residence; Tolkien attended Exeter because of the scholarship he had won. He would also take his degree from Exeter College, Oxford University. However, the requirements for his academic degree, the examinations he would take, and the rules he would live by were all regulated by the university rather than the college. When not on scholarships, students chose colleges because their friends were going to live there, or the rooms were bigger, or the food was better. The academic degree they would win, although awarded by their college, would be no different from those of any other college at the university.

Oxford itself is an old town, steeped in tradition, and during Tolkien's time, many of the centuries-old rules and ideas were still enforced. Tolkien was required to wear his black academic gown at lectures and tutorials, and whenever he went into the town of Oxford itself. Gate hours and cold baths were required. Chapel was compulsory, except for Catholics, Jews, and nonconformists, who were allowed to attend services of their own choosing. Although creature comforts, such as plumbing, were primitive for the most part, the colleges competed at serving the best food and drink. There were many clubs and academic societies, some of them almost as old as the university.

In Tolkien's early years at Oxford, the city had a population of about fifty thousand; about three thousand of these were the junior and senior members of the university. For the most part, the townspeople and the Oxford students and faculty kept apart; they went to different pubs and different restaurants, and students were not encouraged to fraternize romantically with townspeople. Although there were generally peaceful relations between the town and the university, students were urged not to go into dark alleys alone at night in case some resentful citizen might be tempted to renew old rivalries.

At the university, for all the equality of the students, there was still some sharp delineation between students of different backgrounds. *The Lord of the Rings* certainly displays a world governed by a social hierarchy, and many years later, Tolkien remarked, concerning lords and nobility, "I'm rather wedded to these loyalties because I think that, contrary to most people, touching your cap to the squire may be damned bad for the squire, but damned good for you."

Social life at Oxford was delineated by class as well as personality and athletic ability. Socially, a student could be a scholar (someone who studied), a commoner (someone from a good family), or a tosher (someone with a working- or lower-class background). Academically, a student could be a fop (someone who didn't know anything but pretended he knew a great deal) or a swot (someone who really cared for academics). A heartie was an athletic type, friendly and outgoing; an aesthete was "sensitive" and artistically minded. Tolkien was a scholar, a swot, and a heartie.

Many students, especially the commoners, cared little for academics. Practically anybody could get in if he had enough money. In some circles, there was a certain amount of distinction in being awarded a fourth class degree, just barely passing. Some colleges even granted "Grand Compounder" degrees—for a good-sized payment, a student got a degree without ever going to a single class.

Tolkien was chronically short of money. Even though his fees were low by today's standards—the tuition per term was seventy-seven shillings—for him, in his time, things cost a great deal. So for entertainment he would go on long walks with his friends, including a Rhodes scholar from America named Allen Barnett, who introduced Tolkien to his beloved pipe smoking. He and his friends also spent a lot of time in pubs, drinking beer and playing practical jokes on one another. But Tolkien was, for the most part, a scholar, and spent a good deal of time studying.

Tolkien's love of languages was as strong as it had ever been. During his early years at Oxford, he began the serious study of philology. At the encouragement of his first tutor, Joseph Wrighty, Tolkien also began creating and refining his own language, Elvish. He continued to develop the language, and under his other English tutor, world-famous philologist W.A. Craigie, Tolkien learned Icelandic and Finnish, and the myths and folklore of the two countries. Elvish eventually became rooted in Welsh and Finnish.

Tolkien could afford to study other languages because he had chosen not to pursue the general "Greats" or honors classics course which would earn him a B.A. in three years. By studying English instead, he would stay another year at Oxford, and although this would mean additional financial strain—his scholarship would not cover the additional year—it enabled him to explore his other interests. Eventually, Tolkien sat for his final examinations in Moderns, which included Anglo-Saxon rather than Greek and Latin.

His Anglo-Saxon studies had been hampered by the lack of a tutor, but he finally came to study under E.A. Barber, and his old interest in medieval literature was renewed under a New Zealand Rhodes scholar named Kenneth Sisam. These men were important to Tolkien, both because they encouraged him academically and because they gave him a basis for his creation of Elvish. At this time he also realized that in order for any language, including Elvish, to have meaning, there must be a culture and mythology behind it. His first efforts to create a mythology for Elvish took place at Oxford when he began working on stories about the lost continent of Atlantis, which became the island of Númenor in the Second Age of Middle-earth. Tolkien continued work on the Númenor material until 1916, when he abandoned it as "too grim," and began writing the *The Silmarillion.*

By 1914, Tolkien was beginning to think seriously about his future. He still wanted to marry Edith Mary Bratt, but he felt he should have his degree and a fellowship or teaching post before he tried to approach her less-than-enthusiastic relatives. But other events would interfere with his plans—World War I was beginning and thousands of young Englishmen were joining the army. Tolkien was under tremendous pressure to take a commission, yet he wanted to stay at Oxford until he had received his degree.

Between 1914 and 1915, the population of the university dropped from three thousand to one thousand. Tolkien was virtually the only undergraduate left at Exeter College. In 1915, he sat for his final fourth year examinations in English Language and English Literature and received first class honors. On July 7, 1915, he joined the Lancashire Fusiliers. Tolkien, as an Oxford graduate, was automatically awarded an army commission. By the time he had finished his basic training and been awarded the rank of temporary second lieutenant, many of Tolkien's childhood and college friends were dead.

It has been said that an entire generation of England's best young men were lost in the fields of Europe. England was changing, and it would never be the same. At the time when Tolkien joined the army, food was being rationed, there were blackouts in all the major cities, newspapers were censored, and families were being destroyed. War itself had changed. Machine guns mowed down entire ranks of soldiers along the 300-mile battle zone that stretched from the English Channel to the Swiss border. This was a war of attrition, sending in and killing more of the enemy's men than he killed of yours.

Tolkien was very moved by the courage of the common English soldiers. "I've always been impressed that we're here, surviving, because of their indomitable courage against impossible odds." In fact, he once revealed that the most important passage in *The Lord of the Rings* had to do with the small hand that turns the wheel of the world while the larger hand looks away. The small hand turns the world because it has to, and in the same way, the soldiers of World War I went to battle because they had to. Following their example, Tolkien's hobbits went to battle against incredible odds because it was their duty.

On January 8, 1916, Tolkien was transferred to the 11th Battalion of the Lancashire Fusiliers. There were rumors that a final push and breakthrough would occur sometime in the summer, but the Germans had settled in Verdun, and the French, quickly losing men and hope, asked General Field Marshall Haig to advance the plans for a new offensive. Haig chose the Somme River in France as the site of the offensive, though it was an area where such a move was doomed to failure.

Tolkien received word that the fusiliers would leave for the front at the end of March. He took a leave and finally married Edith. After a short honeymoon, Tolkien returned to his battalion and was sent to the front lines in Flanders. Here the men were introduced to trench warfare, with short night marches, and attacks of enemy gas. The fields were a muddy swamp; there were no hot meals, and no washing. There were plenty of lice, colds, snipers, and faulty equipment—and everywhere the smell of death. Although Tolkien has claimed that he did not translate his war experiences into his creative works, the scenes of Frodo's journey through Moria sound like a description of these battlefields. C.S. Lewis, who was a close friend of Tolkien's, has said that the battle scenes in *The Lord of the Rings* "had the very quality of the war my generation knew. . . ."

In April of 1916, Tolkien's battalion was being readied for the barrage that would take place that summer. Everywhere the armies were preparing for battle. Equipment and men were brought in by night, and the British High Command began a propaganda campaign. It was expected that once the Allies had broken through the German trenches, the Germans would have no way of pushing them back.

When the barrage began on June 23rd, Tolkien's battalion was one of those in the British trenches. And his was one of the few that would live to remember the day. In terms of casualities, the battle of

*Bloemfontein, capital of the Orange Free State, South Africa.
Tolkien was born in this frontier city and spent his early childhood there.*

*Mabel Tolkien moved to the Warwickshire village of Sarehole with her two
small children in 1895. Tolkien's rambles through the surrounding countryside aroused a love for English rural life that was later expressed in his
descriptions of the Shire.*

King Edward's School in Birmingham, where the Tolkien brothers were students.

King Edward's School

Exeter College, Oxford. Tolkien won an exhibition scholarship to Exeter in 1911 and graduated from the university in 1915.

C.S. Lewis believed that Tolkien's experiences on the Western Front during World War I were reflected in his vivid descriptions of battle in The Lord of the Rings.

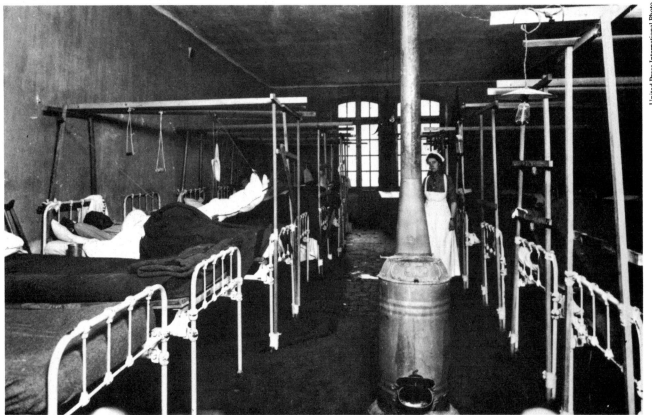

In 1916, Tolkien was evacuated from the front and spent several months recovering from a severe case of trench fever. In a hospital like this one, he began work on The Silmarillion.

W.A. Craigie, editor of the Oxford English Dictionary, *tutored Tolkien at Oxford and later offered him a position as a junior editor on the dictionary.*

Merton College, where Tolkien was Professor of English Language and Literature following World War II.

Tolkien's good friend and fellow Inkling, C.S. Lewis.

A view of Bournemouth, on the southern coast of England. Tolkien and his wife spent their annual holidays at the resort for many years and retired there in 1968.

the Somme was one of the worst in history. All the equipment was useless and in some cases actually a hindrance. The British had brought over the wrong kinds of shells, and their bombardments left the German bunkers and barbed wire virtually untouched. All the equipment slowed the soldiers' advance, and the constant shellings left the field even more muddy and treacherous. As the British soldiers tried to cross the no-man's-land separating the British and German lines, they were mowed down in entire battalions. British casualties that day were fifty thousand men, higher than any other single day of warfare. Communications between bunkers was nonexistent, and those battalions, including Tolkien's, that had managed to move forward and occupy German bunkers were forced to retreat. The battle continued throughout the summer, despite pleas by the field officers that it be ended. Although hailed as a great victory, the Somme was one of the worst military disasters of all time. The British had continued because the casualty reports were so high that they were believed to be exaggerated. By the end of the summer, the Germans and British had each suffered about six hundred thousand casualties. On Nov. 19, 1916, the British stopped the fighting. Almost an entire generation of Britain's manhood had been wiped out.

Tolkien survived the Somme, but he won no medals and received no promotions. In October, as the battle was dying, cold weather descended, and he came down with trench fever. This disease, largely unknown before World War I, is transmitted by lice and fleas. It isn't usually fatal, but causes a high fever and leaves its victims weak and in need of long periods of rest. Tolkien was evacuated to Baupaume in November, and later spent several months recuperating in a military hospital in Birmingham. When he was released, he was never reassigned to a combat battalion.

Tolkien spent his months in the hospital writing what would become *The Silmarillion*. It was set on the same island as his earlier unfinished work, *The Númenor,* and it provided him with the mythology he would need for his Elvish language. The first draft, finished in 1918, had extended the story into the Second Age. Working on his Elvish seemed to settle Tolkien's plans for his future; he decided to return to academic life and study languages.

In 1917, Tolkien was promoted to temporary first lieutenant. When released from the hospital, he did not return to active duty, although he remained attached to the Lancashire Fusiliers. It was an auspicious year for him—he had progressed well with his writing, he had decided on his career, and he had become a father for the first time. He and Edith named their new son John Francis Reuel Tolkien in honor of Father Morgan and Arthur Tolkien.

After Tolkien was released from active service in 1918, he went to work for the Appointments Department of the Ministry of Labor, which handled civilian employment in Britain. Tolkien held this job until the summer of 1919, when he was officially discharged from duty. Although he retained the title of first lieutenant, Tolkien seems to have had no interest in remembering his wartime experiences; in fact, he went to great lengths not to be reminded of them. He never collected the medals and ribbons he was entitled to, and he never applied for the disability award he could have received after his bout with trench fever.

It has been said that the First World War was the turning point in Tolkien's life. In his famous lecture on fairy stories, given in 1938, he remarked that his "real taste for fairy stories was awakened by philology on the threshold of manhood, and quickened to full life by war." Although Tolkien had never been a particularly aggressive man, the war seemed to make him draw into himself; from then on, he did not make close friendships easily, and did not seek fame as a philologist or story writer. Although he certainly deserved it, any success he had seems to have been thrust upon him. He seemed to prefer the quiet life of a teacher and writer to that of a famous lecturer and author. In fact, critic Roger Sale has said that "Tolkien has always spoken . . . as though only fools and madmen would contemplate the twentieth century without horror."

After Tolkien had been discharged from the army, he returned to Oxford. Although he had hoped to receive a fellowship in either Anglo-Saxon or English Literature, competition for positions was fierce, and he worked instead as a substitute teacher and tutor for the English School.

Some of Tolkien's old friends were back at Oxford; after being nearly decimated during the war, the town's population was full of "mature students." These included C.S. Lewis and Gervase Mathew, whom Tolkien had met as a boy on a visit to Gervase's parents, who were friends of Father Francis. Another friend, Nevil Coghill, first met Tolkien when, as secretary of the college essay club, he approached him about delivering a lecture to the group. When asked what he would speak on, Tolkien replied, "the Foragonglin." Tolkien's speech had always been somewhat hurried and mumbling, and it was frequently difficult to understand what he said. Coghill assumed he had said "the Gondolin," and spent a week trying in vain to discover just what it was that Tolkien was going to talk about.

It was about this time that Tolkien attempted to have *The Silmarillion* published, but it was rejected on the grounds that it was too dark and depressing. Tolkien admitted he had doubted that many people would be interested in the work. *The Silmarillion* sat in a drawer untouched until *The Lord of the Rings'* success convinced him to pick it up again.

The work Tolkien had done as an undergraduate at Oxford was remembered by one of his old tutors, W.A. Craigie, one of the four editors of the *Oxford English Dictionary*. Craigie was a professor of Anglo-Saxon, and he knew of Tolkien's work and interests both as a philologist and as an Anglo-Saxon scholar. Craigie offered Tolkien a position on the staff that was preparing what would become the most comprehensive dictionary of the twentieth century. As a junior editor, Tolkien assisted in the selection of approximately two million words and phrases from an available pool of about five million; all this was in continuation of work that had been going on for more than a decade. Tolkien was in his twenties when he began work on the dictionary, and it was a great honor and compliment that anyone as young as he should have held such a position.

Tolkien's work involved both writing definitions and deciding on the origins of the words that had been chosen. In many cases, the sources of particular words were based as much on guessing as on scholarship, and many years later, Tolkien wrote a tale entitled "Farmer Giles of Ham," in which he poked fun at philologists, especially those who had worked on the dictionary. Tolkien's gentle sense of humor, and the way he could both comically and fondly portray the England he knew and loved in his stories, speaks of the combination of scholarship and wit which were so much a part of him.

Tolkien's success and reputation as a scholar continued to grow, and in 1919, he was granted the title of M.A. (Oxon). In England, an M.A. is an honorary title; in some cases, such as Tolkien's, it is granted automatically to graduates of Oxford colleges who have been in residence for five years. It is also awarded to employees and to professors who have been awarded their degrees from other universities. Known as the "Oxbridge M.A.," the title usually means that the person has been elevated from a junior to a senior member of the university. Tolkien had already assumed many responsibilities normally held by a senior member of the university, and the degree gave a certain credibility to the work he had done.

Tolkien was not awarded a higher degree until 1954, when he received his first honorary doctorate. Possibly because of financial responsibilities to his family, Tolkien never enrolled in a doctoral program, and even after he had been awarded his honorary degree, he preferred to use the title of "Professor Tolkien."

In 1920, Tolkien's second son, Michael Hilary Reuel Tolkien, was born. Tolkien's younger brother Hilary, for whom the child was named, was now an apple farmer in the Midlands. Tolkien was still involved with the dictionary, and he spent most of his free time on his own work in Midlands literature, particularly *Beowulf*. Although he was still thought of primarily as a philologist, he was also a highly competent linguist and could speak, read, and write the Romance languages, Welsh and Anglo-Saxon, Finnish and Icelandic, German and Old German, as well as Gothic and a few other obscure languages.

When the work with Craigie on the Oxford dictionary was nearly completed, Tolkien began looking for another position. The University of Leeds had lost a popular professor, F.W. Moorman, in a drowning accident, and there was now a place open in the English department. Tolkien, a philologist and Anglo-Saxon scholar, filled the requirements, and was named Reader of the English Language at the University of Leeds in 1921.

The University of Leeds is in Yorkshire, and Leeds itself is an industrial center. Although originally founded to provide an education in manufacturing and mining, the university gradually lost its heavily industrial orientation and introduced classes in the arts and the classics. It was a prosperous college, funded by the local industry that had originally benefited from the students' training. The English department was heavily oriented toward literature, but during his four years there, Tolkien strengthened its programs in languages and philology. Tolkien was not an administrator, but his ideas and innovations influenced the university's English department for several decades. Tolkien was also in charge of the recently inaugurated doctoral program, even though he did not have the degree himself. He was one of the youngest readers, and was later the youngest professor at the university when he was named one of the two professors in the English Department. Tolkien was Professor of the English Language; the other chair, Professor of English Literature, was held by G.S. Gordon.

The Tolkiens were sociable people, and several of Tolkien's fellow faculty members became lifelong friends. The department of English was small, and the faculty generally very close. Bruce Dickens, a fellow reader, became Professor of the English Language after the death of Tolkien's successor, E.V. Gordon. Another close friend and department member, Lascelles Abercrombie, collaborated with Tolkien until Abercrombie's death in 1938.

Many of Tolkien's honors students became members of the Leeds faculty, or took positions at other universities after the completion of their doctorates. One of his students, E.V. Gordon, would later succeed Tolkien as Professor of the English Language at Leeds. A brilliant philologist and medieval scholar, Gordon received his doctorate while Tolkien was a reader and led an informal study group in medieval Welsh, which Tolkien attended. Gordon later married another of Tolkien's doctoral students, Ida Pickles. Tolkien knew them both as friends and students, and his later work with Gordon would bring him international recognition as a philologist.

Tolkien's earliest work as a philologist had already brought him some fame as a scholar. This was a Middle English vocabulary produced for a book of fourteenth-century verse and prose assembled by his Oxford tutor, Kenneth Sisam. In 1922, Tolkien went on to publish *A Middle English Vocabulary*. However, the work that brought him international fame was his collaboration with E.V. Gordon on a translation of the fourteenth-century work "Sir Gawain and the Green Knight." Sir Gawain, one of the knights of Arthur's Round Table, was the hero of myths dating back to Celtic times. Tolkien had always been fascinated by the Arthurian legend; he had read Mallory's works as a child, and later tried to write his own epic poem of the adventures of Arthur and his knights.

The text Tolkien and Gordon worked on was written by an anonymous fourteenth-century writer whose work was highly literate and contained both English and foreign dialects. There were signs of both Welsh and Irish influence in the highly complex work, which Tolkien and Gordon translated and edited from the original text. Their *Sir Gawain and the Green Knight* was published by the Oxford University Press in 1925. It is still used in most English and

American universities and has become the standard against which all other translations are judged. This work firmly established both Gordon and Tolkien as scholars of Middle English literature, and played a major role in advancing both men's careers. Years later, Tolkien translated the tale into modern English.

Tolkien's relationship with E.V. Gordon, first as a teacher and later as a friend and collaborator, reflects the warm and informal atmosphere at Leeds, especially among professors and upperclassmen. Although the English department held regular meetings, the language specialists would also get together on their own. Tolkien was a regular at these parties, and his knowledge and good humor were a delight to his colleagues. He enjoyed making up songs in Gothic, Icelandic, Scots, and Middle English, and often produced nonsense and satirical verse. When the English Department at University College, London, later published *Songs for the Philologists,* Tolkien's songs were among them.

Tolkien's humor and scholarship combined to make him a popular lecturer. Although Leeds' English department was too small to provide the private tutorials that were so much a part of the Oxford system, Tolkien's lectures were small and informal. He held two-year classes on the old English text of *Beowulf* at Leeds, and would continue to do so at Oxford. He recited the text with great emotion, and the fact that he was often difficult to understand seemed unimportant to some students, although it irritated others. One of his students, J.I.M. Stewart (who later became an Oxford don, and writes popular novels under the name of Michael Innes), declared that Tolkien could "turn a lecture room into a mead hall. . . ." "Tolk," as he was called, was popular and, as David Abercrombie said, "with his striking good looks, his elegance, his wit and his charm, he was, of course, an influential figure as far as his students were concerned."

Tolkien was glad to guide students in need of scholarly advice; he helped them write papers and theses and although some were eventually published, he never took credit for his part. Aware that he was not the most gifted lecturer on the staff, he was always looking for ways to keep his students involved, including concocting Anglo-Saxon crossword puzzles for them. Students were often guests at his house, where they remembered him puffing on his pipe, drinking good quantities of beer, and telling jokes. At home, he enjoyed playing with his two young sons and telling them stories.

His son, Michael, who later became headmaster of a Jesuit boarding school, remembers that, "my father was the only 'grown up' who appeared to take my childish comments and questions with complete seriousness. Whatever interested me interested him more, even my earliest attempts to talk . . . His bedtime stories were exceptional . . . He did not read them from a book, but simply told them, and they were infinitely more exciting and much funnier than anything read from the children's books at the time. That quality of reality, of being inside a story and so being a part of it, which has been, I believe, at least an important factor contributing to the world-wide success of his imaginative works, was already apparent to a small, though already critical and fairly imaginative boy.''

In 1924, Tolkien was made Professor of the English Language at Leeds, and in the same year his third son, Christopher Reuel Tolkien, was born. He and his family enjoyed Leeds, and it proved a productive time both in terms of his work and in helping him to recover from the trauma of the First World War.

But Tolkien's time at Leeds would soon be coming to an end. W.A. Craigie, the man who had helped him to get his position on the *Oxford Dictionary* staff, had been offered a position at the University of Chicago and would be vacating his position at Oxford. By this time, Tolkien's reputation was becoming well established. *Sir Gawain and the Green Knight* had just been published by the Oxford University Press, and the Middle English dictionary he had done in conjunction with Kenneth Sisam was well known. It was only natural that he be considered a candidate for the chair of Bosworth and Rawlinson Professor of Anglo-Saxon. Tolkien was named to the post and left Leeds at the end of the spring term.

The Oxford to which Tolkien returned in 1925 was very different from the Oxford he had known in 1911, or even in 1921. Industry was moving in, and the landscape was being cleared for houses. The traditional influence of the university was fading; Oxford was no longer first a university and only second a city. The university itself was changing. The colleges were more centrally regulated, and new admissions systems encouraged the presence of more working-class students. Women were now admitted to the university, Greek was no longer compulsory, and official proceedings were held in English rather than Latin.

The world itself was changing, as the old England vanished in the wake of the Labor Party, trade unions, and industrialization. As a result, Tolkien drew more and more inside himself and became more comfortable in an atmosphere that was purely academic. His reputation as a scholar was well established, but he felt no great pressure to seek fame or to publish extensively. He and Edith were both attractive people, but their social life soon became limited to family, close friends, and a few students. The Tolkien's moved into a large, red brick house that Tolkien dubbed ''the mansion,'' and there, in 1929, their daughter, Priscilla Anne Reuel Tolkien, was born. Tolkien's role at Oxford was changing as well.

A newly established method for increasing the effectiveness of the Oxford tutorial system required that professors be named fellows of the various colleges. The increasing student population meant that the old system of individual tutorials was less than effective, and by electing professors to colleges, the tutors and professors would work together more closely. Tolkien was elected a fellow of Pembroke College; he held his tutorials there and this was the college with which he was socially connected. His salary was paid by the endowment used to support his professorship.

As he had at Leeds, Tolkien did endless work for faculty projects and contributed to the department's research papers. He also continued his knack for convincing the most brilliant students to join the faculty. One young colleague named Nevil Coghill became a particular protegé. Tolkien helped him to prepare his lectures, and the two became friendly rivals, vying for popularity with the students by reciting anecdotes and humorous literary doggerel.

Coghill eventually became a noted lecturer. The same could not be said for Tolkien; it was his scholarship rather than his style that drew students. His speech was still very difficult to follow, and he mumbled. He also had a habit of wandering off the main subject if something else caught his interest, and many found him difficult to listen to. But the love and inspiration he gave to his students was quite remarkable. Tolkien was generous with his time and knowledge in the hope that his great love of language and mythology would be passed on. In this way he created a bond between himself and his students.

Although Tolkien and his wife were not social whirlwinds, they had a number of close friends. These included Nevil Coghill; Tolkien's childhood friend Gervase Matthew, who had become a don of Balliol College; and some of his English School associates, Professor Dawkins, Helen McMillan Buckhurst, and Professor Hugo Dyson, another expatriate from Leeds.

Dyson, Dawkins, Buckhurst, Coghill, and Tolkien formed a club called the Coalbiters, a name derived from the Icelandic *Kolbitar,* a group of people who huddle around a fire to keep warm. They met in pubs and college rooms, and translated Icelandic sagas for each other. Tolkien was particularly skilled at this. As with many such groups, the Coalbiters slowly faded, but for a time the club provided Tolkien and his friends with a friendly audience for their work.

Perhaps Tolkien's closest friend, the man most like him in spirit as well as in love of scholarship, was Clive Staple Lewis. Lewis had attended Oxford, but his studies were interrupted by World War I. When he returned after the war, he was unable to get a fellowship in philosophy, so he prepared instead for a fellowship in English. He had studied Anglo-Saxon as an undergraduate, and in 1925 he became a fellow in the department of English Language and Literature.

Lewis had a wide variety of interests. He was one of a group known as the "Oxford Christians," and although he had never been formally converted, as Tolkien had, his atheistic tendencies had been shattered by what he termed "the facts." Lewis loved smoking a pipe, drinking beer, and discussing mythology and poetry. He also shared Tolkien's great sense of humor. Lewis has been said to have resembled one of Tolkien's hobbits. Both he and Tolkien hated to be interrupted or disagreed with, and could become very angry when irritated.

Jocelyn Hill describes Lewis' preeminent quality as "an unshakable deep sense of truth." Lewis gained the broad popularity that Tolkien shunned; his children's books and radio broadcasts made him a popular figure. Although he seemed more a citizen of the modern world than his friend, he also shared Tolkien's love of fantasy. One story tells of Tolkien and Lewis talking intently in a pub for what seemed like hours. When someone asked Lewis what they were talking about, he replied, "Dragons," and immediately returned to the discussion.

Tolkien was surrounded by a warm group of friends. Owen Barfield, whom Lewis described as "unable to talk on any subject without illuminating it," shared Tolkien's love for the countryside. Every spring, he and Tolkien would join a group to take long walks through the woods and fields. Barfield had the contradictory nature common to many of Tolkien's compatriots; he could be very friendly or very aloof. He loved to talk on a wide variety of subjects, and he could argue a cause quite intensely, even if no one else was acquainted with the subject.

Tolkien was devoted to these good friends. Without their encouragement, support, and shared interest in mythology, *The Lord of the Rings* might never have been written. Although his friends encouraged him, and his scholarly pursuits were the foundation of his creative work, the writing of his most famous works came about in a peculiar way. Tolkien always seemed to be suffering from financial worries. He had considerable expenses—children who had to be educated and a large house to support—and professors at Oxford, although paid more than most other professors at English universities, still earned much less than their American counterparts. Tolkien's problem was not so much a lack of money as the fact that no matter how much he earned, he would always have liked to be earning just a little bit more. Unlike Lewis, who was a prolific writer and lecturer, Tolkien needed to find a way to supplement his income. He took a job grading Oxford's entrance examinations.

One day in 1928, Tolkien came across an exam with a blank sheet of paper in it. "One of the candidates mercifully left one of the sheets with no writing on it—which is possibly the best thing that can happen to an examiner—and I wrote on it 'In a hole in the ground lived a hobbit.' Names always generate a story in my mind and eventually I thought I should find out what hobbits were like. But that was only the beginning; I spun the elements out of my head; I didn't do any organizing at all."

There are conflicting reports about the exact year in which *The Hobbit* was begun. Tolkien graded papers until the '30s, and he himself believed it was much later that he found the blank sheet of paper. But his son, Michael, was sure that he was seven when he first heard about hobbits, and he would have been seven in 1928. Possibly Tolkien was referring to the date when *The Hobbit* was first written as a manuscript, which was years later.

The origin of the word "hobbit" is not known; Tolkien said he wasn't sure where it came from. Edmund Wilson believed it was a combination of "rabbit" and (Thomas) "Hobbes." Paul Kocher, in his work *Master of Middle Earth,* speculates that the word is derived from the Middle English "hob," meaning clown or rustic. Tolkien *was* sure that he did not intend the hobbits to be tiny. "I don't like small creatures," he said. "Hobbits are three to four feet in height. You can see people like that."

The ideas for the book itself seem to have come slowly and then grown as he went along. Tolkien first presented *The Hobbit* as a children's book. "If you're a youngish man and you don't want to be made fun of, you say you're writing for children. At any rate, children are your immediate audience and you write or tell them stories for which they are mildly grateful: long, rambling stories at bedtime." As to the style of writing, which some people have called simplistic and childish, Tolkien replied, *"The Hobbit* was written in what I should now regard as bad style, as if one were talking to children. There's nothing my children loathed more. They taught me a lesson. Anything that in any way marked *The Hobbit* out as for children instead of just people, they disliked—instinctively. I did too, now that I think about it."

If Tolkien did not write the book simply for children, why did he write it? Nevil Coghill thought it was for money. It is more probable, though, that Tolkien was even then embarking on his attempt to make a modern myth, something that would connect the past, the England he loved so dearly, with the modern world he saw. He would later say that his purpose in *The Lord of the Rings* was "to modernize the myths and make them credible." As a philologist, Tolkien was fascinated by language as a foundation for myth and the development of culture. In writing *The Hobbit* and *The Lord of the Rings,* he was inspired by the Norse legends; many of the names in his tales come from *The Elder Edda.* "I gave the dwarfs actual Norse names which are in Norse books," said Tolkien. "Not that my dwarfs are really like the dwarfs of Norse imagination, but there is a whole list of attractive dwarf names in one of the old epic poems." Mirkwood forest appears in an Icelandic saga, *King Heidrek the Wise,* Gandalf's name appears in *Halfdan the Black,* and Middle-earth is an ancient name for our own world.

The life he had led and the things he loved obviously show through in Tolkien's work. But his writing was not simply an emotional response to this influence. Much of his writing is also directly linked to his interest in language and mythology. He found something deeply personal in the study of language. "People have linguistic predilections, but like one's physical characteristics, they shift as you grow, also as you have more experience. In language, I've tried to fit my actual personal predilection or pleasure."

Tolkien's interest in *The Hobbit* was an on-and-off affair. A handwritten draft circulated among friends in the 1930s, but was not sent off for publication, even though he was urged to do so. Perhaps, he feared the ridicule of his colleagues; or perhaps he was so modest that he feared the popularity success might bring him. Or perhaps he was too preoccupied with another, more scholarly project.

Tolkien was an acknowledged authority on *Beowulf.* When he won a Leverhulme scholarship in 1936, designed to allow professors not on sabbatical to pursue independent research subjects, it is likely that he devoted his attention to *Beowulf*. He had long felt that people had lost sight of the story by concentrating too much attention on its supposed meanings. In 1936, Tolkien spoke at the annual lecture at the British Academy on the subject of *Beowulf: The Monsters and the Critics*. In his lecture, which is considered to be the finest discussion of Anglo-Saxon literature in this century, Tolkien began by making fun of the critics. "For it is of their nature that the jabberwocks of historical and antiquarian research burble in the tulgy wood of conjecture. . . ." Of monsters, he said, "It is the strength of the northern mythological imagination that . . . put them in the center, gave them victory but no honor, and found a potent but terrible solution in naked will and courage. . . . So potent is it, that while the older southern imagination has faded forever in literary ornament, the northern has power, as it were, to revive its spirit even in our own times."

Tolkien's portrayal of monsters in both *The Hobbit* and *The Lord of the Rings* is an effective use of darker elements to allude to a darker and even richer past. Tolkien's lecture on *Beowulf* was a work of both scholarship and feeling, for its themes concerned him deeply. *Beowulf: The Monsters and the Critics* was published by the Oxford University Press and included in an anthology of *Beowulf* criticism in 1963. It was published even more recently as a Folcroft book. From its first appearance, the acclaim it received established Tolkien's scholarly reputation.

As Tolkien's credentials as a philologist were beginning to be truly established, so too was his fame as an author. Many of his friends had read the manuscript of *The Hobbit*, yet Tolkien left it sitting in a drawer. One colleague, Elaine Griffiths, had a friend named Susan Dagnell who worked for a small publishing house in London. Susan, a most persuasive woman, managed to get the manuscript away from Tolkien, who allowed her to submit it to her employers, George Allen and Unwin. She gave it to the chairman of the board, Sir Stanley Unwin, who in turn gave it to his son, Rayner, aged ten. Rayner Unwin frequently read children's books for his father and was paid from a shilling to half a crown for reviewing them. His report on *The Hobbit*, dated Oct. 30, 1936, urged publication. Rayner later remarked, "I wouldn't say my report was the best critique of *The Hobbit* that was ever written, but it was good enough to ensure that it was published."

The Hobbit, published in 1937, received excellent reviews. The *London Times* wrote:

> All who love that kind of children's book which can be read and re-read by adults should note that a new star has appeared in this constellation. . . . in this book, a number of good things, never before united, have come together: a fund of humor, an understanding of children, and a happy fusion of the scholar's with the poet's grasp of mythology. On the edge of a valley one of Professor Tolkien's characters can pause and say: "It smells like elves." It may be years before we produce another author with such a nose for an elf. The professor has an air of inventing nothing. He has studied trolls and dragons at first hand and

describes them with the fidelity which is worth oceans of glib "originality".

The New Statesman and Nation said, "his wholly original story of adventure among goblins, elves and dragons . . . gives . . . the impression of a well-informed glimpse into the life of a wide other-world; a world wholly real, and with a quite matter-of-fact, supernatural history of its own."

With the publication of *The Hobbit* in 1937, Tolkien began to emerge from his self-imposed isolation. He had previously been recognized by his peers as a scholar and teacher, but with the *Beowulf* lectures and then *The Hobbit*, his reputation spread beyond his own small circle.

C.S. Lewis and J.R.R. Tolkien were close friends and helped each other in their literary endeavors. Tolkien criticized, and Lewis encouraged. Both men were, in fact, members of a group which gave its members the same kind of help the two friends gave each other.

The Inklings met at Oxford from the 1930s until the early 1960s. Neither Tolkien nor Lewis founded the group, but Lewis soon became its most prominent member. The Inklings had far-ranging discussions on a variety of topics, including their works in progress. The club was informal in nature; there were no regular meetings and no budgets or rules, at least no explicit ones. The members found that they had become a group more than that they had agreed to become one. They would meet on Thursdays or Fridays in various pubs scattered around Oxford, usually in a back room where they could drink and talk without interruption.

The Inklings' meetings changed somewhat over the years. What had begun as a kind of joke by an undergraduate named Tangye-Lean, who invited several dons to his rooms to discuss literature, emerged as a group of C.S. Lewis' admirers and friends. Lewis, Tolkien, and novelist Charles Williams were the most famous members in that they had readers and admirers outside their scholastic circle. Most of the other members were distinguished in their chosen fields.

Members came and went, but a few of the regulars included Nevil Coghill, who would follow Tolkien as Merton Professor of English Language and Literature, and Hugo Dyson, who, although he had left Oxford shortly after Tolkien returned, kept a summer position at the English School and so remained in contact with the university and his friends. Owen Barfield became a member, commuting from London at the beginning of each term to see his close friend C.S. Lewis. One of the few Inkling rules emerged on one occasion when Barfield brought along a friend without informing the other members that he was doing so; the guest was never invited back.

Charles Williams was one of the more unusual Inklings. His father had been an impoverished poet, and Williams had no formal education beyond several terms at the University of London. Beginning as an assistant clerk, Williams worked his way up to become head of the Oxford University Press. He was creative, widely read, and a prolific writer.

Although all the Inklings were devout Christians, Williams, Tolkien, and Lewis were the three most prominent exponents of their beliefs. Williams' spirituality came through in all he did; for him, the real and the spiritual world were one. Lewis once said that although Williams "was a rather ugly man . . . after he has begun speaking, his face becomes angelic." T.S. Eliot remarked that "while his novels are constantly flashing with religious insight, his religious books communicate a good deal of the excitement of a sensational novel."

Tolkien, Lewis, and Williams all became well known for their advocacy of Christian morals and theology. Dr. Clyde Kilby of Wheaton College, who knew Tolkien and worked with him, has said the three men "found a system of cosmic order and 'created a myth to contain it.'" Tolkien, Lewis, and Williams loved to discuss metaphysics and theology. Both Lewis and Williams frequently spoke and wrote about their Anglican religion, but Tolkien never did so. Despite this, Christianity was an important part of Tolkien's life; indeed, in describing the Inklings and the support they gave his literary efforts, he once said, "What I owe them is incalculable. . . . Is there any pleasure on earth as great as the circle of Christian friends by a good fire?"

Although one of the primary purposes of the Inklings was to criticize new works by its members, Tolkien had a very difficult time accepting this advice. According to Lewis, Tolkien had "two reactions to criticism; either he begins the whole thing over from the beginning or else he takes no notice at all." Tolkien, however, related that it was not the criticism, but the manner that had an effect. "Whenever he said, 'You can do better than that. Better, Tolkien, please,' I used to try."

It's no use denying that Tolkien could be a stubborn man. When his publishers pointed out that "dwarves" was actually spelled "dwarfs," using the *Oxford English Dictionary* as its source, Tolkien not only refused to change it, but added, "After all, I *wrote* the *Oxford English Dictionary*." Later he admitted that "of course, dwarves is originally a mistake in grammar, and I tried to cover it up."

Tolkien and Lewis met frequently on their own to discuss, to encourage, and to argue. One of their favorite topics of conversation was allegory—Lewis was a proponent, and Tolkien was adamantly against it. His dislike of allegory was rooted in both his belief in the value of personal interpretation and his dislike of domination, critical or otherwise. In the Ballantine edition of *The Lord of the Rings*, he wrote, "I cordially dislike allegory in all its manifestations, and always have done so since I grew old and wary enough to detect its presence. I much prefer history, true or feigned, with its varied applicability to the thought and experience of the readers. I think that many confuse applicability with allegory; but the one resides in the freedom of the reader, and the other in the domination of the author.'' When discussing the trilogy in an interview he said, "It has *no* allegorical intentions, general, particular, or topical, moral, religious, or political.''

One of these meetings with Lewis, an evening in 1937 when the Inklings did not meet, provides the earliest record of Tolkien's work on *The Lord of the Rings*. Lewis recalled Tolkien reading a chapter from the "new Hobbit"; he would continue to read revisions and new chapters of his work to friends for the next fourteen years.

The Inklings helped to shape *The Lord of the Rings*, not through any direct criticism but rather through their encouragement to continue the work. During these years Tolkien himself seemed to have formulated his views on fantasy. These were presented in a lecture given in 1938, at the University of St. Andrews in Scotland entitled, "On Fairy-Stories." This is probably Tolkien's most famous lecture; in it, he described the role and need for fairy stories in modern life, and then went on to present the formula for a successful modern mythology. Tolkien spoke of the need to escape from the troubles of our modern world into another world where even wizards and dragons were much more appealing, and where good and evil were more simply and clearly defined.

Tolkien emphasized that this turn to fantasy was not so much a desire to escape from this world as it was a desire to use the fantasy world to create a better reality. The created world must follow the world of reality so that the reader may find the new world believable. It may have dragons and wizards, but the fantasy must be consistent and believable. In his book, *Master of Middle-earth,* Paul Kocher describes this quality. "The reader walks through any Middle-earth landscape with a security of recognition that woos him on to believe anything that happens. Familiar but not too familiar, strange but not too strange. This is the master rubric that Tolkien bears always in mind when creating the world of the epic."

Tolkien believed that the fantasy writer must present himself as not so much the creator as the sub-creator, the rediscoverer of an old world rather than the inventor of a new one. By doing this, the world he creates will seem like one which has passed by, but did indeed exist at one time. By remaining consistent with the laws of nature familiar to the reader, the writer is able to make the new mythology part of the reader's own world and experience.

Tolkien's lecture on fairy stories and the beginning of his work on *The Lord of the Rings* marked the beginning of a period of happiness and success. In 1938, his son John went to Exeter College, Michael went to Trinity the following year, and Christopher went to Trinity before being commissioned in the R.A.F. in 1942. During these years, Tolkien continued work upon the "new Hobbit," and also wrote a fairy story called "Leaf by Niggle." Tolkien was also appointed coeditor of the Oxford English Monograph series, supervising a number of books of Nordic and Anglo-Saxon literature being published by the Oxford University Press. C.S. Lewis was one of the other editors, and this is one of the few times he and Tolkien worked together. In the 1950s, they began collaborating on a book, but Tolkien procrastinated so much that Lewis gave up the project.

Tolkien's work on *The Lord of the Rings* began soon after George Allen and Unwin decided to publish *The Hobbit* in 1936. Tolkien has said that he began writing *The Lord of the Rings* as a test of his ability to sustain a reader's interest for a fairly long length of time. He liked the idea of a pilgrimage with an ultimate goal, and decided that the ring in *The Hobbit* would be a suitable device for such a plot. The ring linked the stories, and would continue the characters of Bilbo, Gandalf, Gollum, and the hobbits. Tolkien later tightened certain parts of *The Hobbit* so that the two stories would be more harmonious.

Work on *The Lord of the Rings* was different from that which had been involved in *The Hobbit*. *The Hobbit* was really a transcription of stories Tolkien had told his children, and he had them published only after a great deal of encouragement and urging. When he began work on the new book, it was not as a children's story, and he did not look to children for criticism. The Inklings, grown men with strongly scholastic bents, listened and criticized the story during the course of its writing. Tolkien has said that the story "grew without control, except a major one that the ring had to be destroyed, which came out quite early through Gandalf. Several times I tried to write that last scene ahead of time, but it didn't quite come out, never worked."

The Lord of the Rings was also a continuation of Tolkien's search for a mythology for his Elvish language. "The invention of language is the foundation," he said. "The stories were made rather to provide a world for the language than the reverse." Tolkien once admitted that he had considered writing the entire book in Elvish, but much of the original Elvish was edited out. "Only as much language has been left in as I thought would be stomached by readers." The language came first with him, and the mythology provided its framework and history. For the reader, however, Tolkien had to "get across a whole mythology which I've invented before you get down to the stories."

Middle-earth, Tolkien said, "is simply an old-fashioned word for the world we live in, as imagined and surrounded by the ocean . . . at a different stage of imagination." An historical time frame, however, "would be impossible, because it was completely interfered with and trampled by the free invention of history and incidents of one's own story."

The Lord of the Rings does, however, contain bits of Tolkien's historical knowledge. Middle-earth resembles "some of the history of Greece and Rome as against the perpetual infiltration of people from the east." Many parts of the story are influenced by the *Elder Edda*, the original source of Norse mythology. Much of Tolkien's private life came into the book as well. The ents, for example, were the result of a request from his son Michael, who had seen trees being cut down and thought of this as the murder of living things. He asked his father to "make up a tale in which the trees took a terrible revenge on the machine lovers." Priscilla, Tolkien's daughter, had a doll named Tom; so into the story came Tom Bombadil.

Many details in *The Lord of the Rings* come directly from the world as we know it. Tolkien's characters have possessions "including tobacco, umbrellas, and things little known to archeological history." Allen Barnett, Tolkien's friend from Kentucky, told him stories of the mountain people back home and so contributed to Tolkien's portrayal of the hobbits. Tolkien tried to be as precise as possible—the moon cycles in the trilogy are those which occurred in 1942; for measure of a long march, Tolkien turned to a British army ordnance manual.

Tolkien began *The Lord of the Rings* in 1937; he worked on it for eleven years before he had completed the first draft. During this period, the Inklings provided encouragement and gave him hope. He seriously considered abandoning the manuscript on at least two occasions, and it is doubtful whether he would ever have completed it without the Inklings' support. The first edition of *The Lord of the Rings* was dedicated to the Tolkien children, and to "the Inklings, because they have already listened to it with a patience, and indeed with an interest that almost leads me to suspect that they have hobbit-blood in their venerable ancestry."

Tolkien finished most of Book I in 1939. The shock of World War II temporarily halted the work, and after that he progressed slowly and sporadically. During the next five years, he wrote little by little. Tolkien abhorred war. Over and above the psychic horror he shared with many others, Tolkien suffered personally in ways which, though they seem small, made him uncomfortable and uneasy. Rationing meant an end to his supplies of tobacco and beer, and wartime food gave him stomach ulcers. His sons Michael and Christopher both joined the R.A.F.; John was about to join the priesthood.

Oxford had changed drastically as well. When the war broke out, the university had an enormous enrollment of 5,000. Many of the staff and students went off to join the war, and Tolkien soon found himself the head of the English faculty. In this new atmosphere Tolkien found it difficult to write. He had added responsibilities, and the war proved mentally and physically debilitating. It was not until Christopher was sent to South Africa that Tolkien was able to resume his work, mailing chapters to his son as he completed them. It was five years, however, before the story was finished.

The long delays in the completion of *The Lord of the Rings* were due in part to other changes in Tolkien's life both during and after the war. Between 1945 and 1948, Tolkien gave up his seat as Bosworth and Rawlinson Professor of Anglo-Saxon, the position he had held for twenty years, after being offered the chair of Merton Professor of English Language and Literature. Although Tolkien had begun his career as a philologist, his work on *Beowulf* and his lecture on fairy stories had established him as a literary scholar as well. In accepting the Merton chair, Tolkien also gave up his connections with Pembroke College and became a member of Merton College. He also changed his family residence. By this time only one of the Tolkiens' children, their daughter Priscilla, was living at home, and the house was too big and expensive to maintain. As a result, they moved to a small Victorian house belonging to the university.

Tolkien's family had all survived the war. John had been ordained and was working in the bombed-out city of Coventry. Both Michael and Christopher returned to Trinity College, and Priscilla went to Lady Margaret Hall, Oxford, in 1948. Tolkien had been offered a post for a year at the Catholic University in Washington, but Edith's health was poor, and he could not afford to go by himself and continue to support his wife and daughter in England.

The final draft of *The Lord of the Rings* was completed in 1949, and Tolkien submitted it to George Allen and Unwin in 1950. Rayner Unwin, who as a boy had urged his father to publish *The Hobbit*, was now a member of the firm. He had been at Oxford and had visited Tolkien, so he was aware of the professor's progress on *The Lord of the Rings*. Unfortunately, when Tolkien submitted his manuscript, it was read by a stranger and rejected. Tolkien was heartbroken. He stuck the manuscript away in a drawer and despite the urgings of friends, refused to send it out. Instead, he worked on several shorter pieces, including a poetic version of a battle between the English and the Danes called *The Battle of Maldon* and an epic about St. Brendan sailing from Ireland to Europe entitled *Imran*.

Tolkien continued to keep his creative energies focused on other things, even though friends begged him to resubmit *The Lord of the Rings*. When he finally did so, one publisher told him that it was unsaleable, and another wanted him to make drastic revisions. He even considered this last possibility—he was just sixty, approaching retirement age, and his financial difficulties always haunted him. He had moved once more, and wanted to live out his days in some peace and security.

The Lord of the Rings might have been lost if Rayner Unwin had not heard about the rejection and insisted that Tolkien resubmit the work to him personally. When Unwin received it, he concluded that it was a work of genius and cabled his father, who was traveling abroad, asking for directions. Sir Stanley Unwin was brief, yet he said the right thing: IF YOU THINK IT A WORK OF GENIUS THEN YOU MAY LOSE £1,000. Although it doesn't seem like much today, £1,000 was a great deal of money for the time, and for a publishing house the size of Allen and Unwin. Since the manuscript could not be cut, it was decided to divide the book into three parts. One volume might sell better than another, and there would not be such a large cash outlay at one time.

At first, Tolkien objected to splitting up the book, but when Unwin gave his reasons he acquiesced. Allen & Unwin then commissioned three writers to give their impressions of the book. One was Tolkien's old friend, C.S. Lewis, who wrote, "Here are beauties which pierce like swords or burn like cold iron; here is a book that will break your heart . . . good beyond hope." It appeared that most people agreed with him—the book was an immediate success.

Tolkien's literary success was preceded by acclaim as a scholar.

In 1954, he received honorary degrees from University College, Dublin, and the University of Liège in Belgium. He delivered several speeches, and was elected Vice President of the Philological Society of Great Britain. Tolkien had waited a long time for such international recognition, but he finally seemed to be getting the fame he deserved.

The success of *The Lord of the Rings* even enabled Tolkien to buy a new house. Tolkien's children were all grown. John was the Catholic priest at Keele University, and Michael had become a master at a Benedictine School in Yorkshire. Christopher was a fellow and later a lecturer in Old English at Oxford, and Priscilla was soon to become a teacher at a technological school in Oxford. Christopher and Michael were both married and had children, and Tolkien adored his grandchildren, who called him "Grandfellow." Unfortunately, Edith's poor health continued, and Tolkien was unable to go to the United States to receive the honorary degrees both Harvard and Marquette had bestowed upon him.

The years of 1957 and 1958 were a period of transition for Tolkien; his fame as a writer was really just beginning, and his career as a scholar was coming to an end. In 1957, he received his first literary award for *The Lord of the Rings*, and he continued to be sought after to give speeches and lectures. But Tolkien was growing old, and drawing more and more into his reclusive ways. In 1958, he retired from his professorship at Oxford. Both Merton and Exeter Colleges awarded him with honorary fellowships, and his valedictory assembly at Merton College Hall was packed.

As a Professor Emeritus, Tolkien continued his private research and scholarly writings. In addition, *The Lord of the Rings* continued to sell well, and his publishers produced a collection of poetry from the trilogy called *The Adventures of Tom Bombadil*. The furor which *The Lord of the Rings* had originally caused appeared to be easing off, and Tolkien's life seemed fairly settled.

In 1965, however, everything changed drastically. A copyright disagreement disclosed the fact that *The Lord of the Rings* had fallen into the public domain in America, and an unauthorized paperback edition was scheduled to be released by Ace Books. At this, an "authorized" paperback version was quickly scheduled by Ballantine Books.

Within a year, Ace had sold 200,000 copies of the trilogy, and that in competition with Ballantine. Despite this, Ace received adverse publicity, and it decided to suspend publication of the trilogy. Ballantine, now left with the market to itself, not only took over Ace's share, but suddenly found itself owning a roaring best seller. After a brief lull between the original edition in the 1950s and the paperback editions in 1965, the book became a hit at campuses across the United States. Tolkien's publishers estimated that by the end of 1968, more than 50 million people throughout the world had read his book.

Tolkien had become a cult figure. Mail poured into his publishers, and packages and fan letters came from all over the world. In 1967, *The Lord of the Rings* was being published in nine languages, and Tolkien's privacy was being threatened by requests for autographs, and letters, and even old pipes. The formerly money-troubled Tolkien was now complaining about his high taxes. Toy companies and moviemakers besieged him with offers.

Tolkien asked Allen & Unwin to help him deal with his new-found public. A young woman named Joy Hill was sent to be his secretary and organizer, but even with her help, life at Oxford had become impossible. The Tolkiens decided to leave the city, and in great quiet and secrecy they moved to Bournemouth. No one in the area knew who they were, only that they were "famous." Great precautions were taken to ensure the Tolkiens' privacy, and Joy Hill was their primary contact with the outside world.

In 1972, after a long illness, Edith died. She had been married to Tolkien for fifty-five years, and he was profoundly grieved. His children tried to ease his great loneliness, but the task was not easy.

After friends threw an eightieth birthday party for him at Oxford, Tolkien decided to return to Merton College. He later said that "it was like returning to a metropolis from a desert island." Merton College was also very pleased to have Tolkien back. Everyone took a great interest in his health and welfare, and he dined regularly with the rest of the college. Unfortunately, Tolkien was still somewhat lonely, and he began visiting old peoples' clubs in the area. Charles and Mavis Carr, the college servants, also helped give Tolkien the companionship he missed.

Even in retirement, Tolkien continued to receive honors. In 1972, Oxford awarded him an honorary Doctor of Literature degree; it was the fourth of the five he would receive, and the academic honor which meant the most to him. In 1973 he was presented the Order of the British Empire by Queen Elizabeth. The last prize he received was from the French, as the best foreign writer in 1973. Unfortunately, he was ill and unable to go to Paris to receive the award in person.

Although Tolkien was getting old, his health was good. His only difficulties came from eating too much rich food and from the damp Oxford weather. Although Tolkien continued to try to work, he was a procrastinator by nature: perhaps he sensed that he would not live to see his final work, *The Silmarillion*, completed.

Later in the summer of 1973, Tolkien had lunch with his daughter Priscilla. The next morning, he got on the train to visit friends in Bournemouth. As Carr wished him goodbye, Tolkien remarked, "I feel on top of the world." Five days later, he died of pneumonia, complicated by a gastric ulcer, in a Bournemouth hospital.

Elven Warrior

Over the past twenty-five years, J.R.R. Tolkien has become a respected figure in the literary world. But this wasn't always the case. When the final volume of The Lord of the Rings *appeared, it provoked a great deal of debate among literary critics. Was Tolkien's trilogy just a passing fancy, the sort of bestseller huge audiences would read and set aside when the next fad came along? Or was it a work of genius, a classic destined to be enjoyed by generations? With perfect hindsight, many of us would find the answer obvious, but in 1956, when the following exchange occurred between two of America's leading men of letters, the lines were not so clearly drawn.*

At the End of the Quest, Victory

by W. H. Auden

In "The Return of the King," Frodo Baggins fulfills his Quest, the realm of Sauron is ended forever, the Third Age is over and J.R.R. Tolkien's trilogy "The Lord of the Rings" complete. I rarely remember a book about which I have had such violent arguments. Nobody *seems* to have a moderate opinion: either, like myself, people find it a masterpiece of its genre or they cannot abide it, and among the hostile there are some, I must confess, for whose literary judgment I have great respect. A few of these may have been put off by the first forty pages of the first chapter of the first volume in which the daily life of the hobbits is described; this is light comedy and light comedy is not Mr. Tolkien's forte. In most cases, however, the objection must go far deeper. I can only suppose that some people object to Heroic Quests and Imaginary Worlds on principle; such, they feel, cannot be anything but light "escapist" reading. That a man like Mr. Tolkien, the English philologist who teaches at Oxford, should lavish such incredible pains upon a genre which is, for them, trifling by definition, is, therefore, very shocking.

The difficulty of presenting a complete picture of reality lies in the gulf between the subjectively real, a man's experience of his own existence, and the objectively real, his experience of the lives of others and the world about him. Life, as I experience it in my own person, is primarily a continuous succession of choices between alternatives, made for a short-term or long-term purpose; the actions I take, that is to say, are less significant to me than the conflicts of motives, temptations, doubts in which they originate. Further, my subjective experience of time is not of a cyclical motion outside myself but of an irreversible history of unique moments which are made by my decisions.

For objectifying this experience, the natural image is that of a journey with a purpose, beset by dangerous hazards and obstacles, some merely difficult, others actively hostile. But when I observe my fellow men, such an image seems false. I can see, for example, that only the rich and those on vacation can take journeys; most men, most of the time must work in one place.

I cannot observe them making choices, only the actions they take and, if I know someone well, I can usually predict correctly how he will act in a given situation. I observe, all too often, men in conflict with each other, wars and hatreds, but seldom, if ever, a clear-cut issue between Good on the one side and Evil on the other, though I also observe that both sides usually describe it as such. If, then, I try to describe what I see as if I were an impersonal camera, I shall produce, not a Quest, but a "naturalistic" document.

Both extremes, of course, falsify life. There are medieval Quests which deserve the criticism made by Erich Auerbach in his book "Mimesis":

> The world of knightly proving is a world of adventure. It not only contains a practically uninterrupted series of adventures; more specifically, it contains nothing but the requisites of adventure * * * Except feats of arms and love, nothing occurs in the courtly world—and even these two are of a special sort: they are not occurrences or emotions which can be absent for a time; they are permanently connected with the person of the perfect knight, they are part of his definition, so that he cannot for one moment be without adventure in arms nor for one moment without amorous entanglement * * * His exploits are feats of arms, not 'war,' for they are feats accomplished at random which do not fit into any politically purposive pattern.

And there are contemporary "thrillers" in which the identification of hero and villain with contemporary politics is depressingly obvious. On the other hand, there are naturalistic novels in which the characters are the mere puppets of Fate, or rather, of the author who, from some mysterious point of freedom, contemplates the workings of Fate.

If, as I believe, Mr. Tolkien has succeeded more completely than any previous writer in this genre in using the traditional properties of the Quest, the heroic journey, the Numinous Object, the conflict between Good and Evil while at the same time satisfying our sense of historical and social reality, it should be possible to show how he has succeeded. To begin with, no previous writer has, to my knowledge, created an imaginary world and a feigned history in such detail. By the time the reader has finished the trilogy, including the appendices to this last volume, he knows as much about Mr.

Tolkien's Middle-earth, its landscape, its fauna and flora, its peoples, their languages, their history, their cultural habits, as, outside his special field, he knows about the actual world.

Mr. Tolkien's world may not be the same as our own: it includes, for example, elves, beings who know good and evil but have not fallen, and, though not physically indestructible, do not suffer natural death. It is afflicted by Sauron, an incarnation of absolute evil, and creatures like Shelob, the monster spider, or the orcs who are corrupt past hope of redemption. But it is a world of intelligible law, not mere wish; the reader's sense of the credible is never violated.

Even the One Ring, the absolute physical and psychological weapon which must corrupt any who dares to use it, is a perfectly plausible hypothesis from which the political duty to destroy it which motivates Frodo's Quest logically follows.

To present the conflict between Good and Evil as a war in which the good side is ultimately victorious is a ticklish business. Our historical experience tells us that physical power and, to a large extent, mental power are morally neutral and effectively real: wars are won by the stronger side, just or unjust. At the same time most of us believe that the essence of the Good is love and freedom so that Good cannot impose itself by force without ceasing to be good.

The battles in the Apocalypse and "Paradise Lost," for example, are hard to stomach because of the conjunction of two incompatible notions of Deity, of a God of Love who creates free beings who can reject his love and of a God of absolute Power whom none can withstand. Mr. Tolkien is not as great a writer as Milton, but in this matter he has succeeded where Milton failed. As readers of the preceding volumes will remember, the situation in the War of the Ring is as follows: Chance, or Providence, has put the Ring in the hands of the representatives of Good, Elrond, Gandalf, Aragorn. By using it they could destroy Sauron, the incarnation of Evil, but at the cost of becoming his successor. If Sauron recovers the Ring, his victory will be immediate and complete, but even without it his power is greater than any his enemies can bring against him, so that, unless Frodo succeeds in destroying the Ring, Sauron must win.

Evil, that is, has every advantage but one—it is inferior in imagination. Good can imagine the possibility of becoming evil—hence the refusal of Gandalf and Aragorn to use the Ring—but Evil, defiantly chosen, can no longer imagine anything but itself. Sauron cannot imagine any motives except lust for dominion and fear so that, when he has learned that his enemies have the Ring, the thought that they might try to destroy it never enters his head, and his eye is kept turned toward Gondor and away from Mordor and the Mount of Doom.

Further, his worship of power is accompanied, as it must be, by anger and a lust for cruelty: learning of Saruman's attempt to steal the Ring for himself, Sauron is so preoccupied with wrath that for two crucial days he pays no attention to a report of spies on the stairs of Cirith Ungol, and when Pippin is foolish enough to look in the palantir of Orthanc, Sauron could have learned all about Frodo's Quest. His wish to capture Pippin and torture the truth from him makes him miss his precious opportunity.

Sauron is not overthrown, however, before many brave men have died and much damage has been done and even his defeat involves loss—the three Elven Rings lose their power and the Elves must leave Middle-earth. Nor is the victory of Good over Evil final: there was Morgoth before Sauron and no one knows what dread successor may afflict the world in ages to come.

The demands made on the writer's powers in an epic as long as "The Lord of the Rings" are enormous and increase as the tale proceeds—the battles have to get more spectacular, the situations more critical, the adventures more thrilling—but I can only say that Mr. Tolkien has proved equal to them. Readers of the previous volumes may be interested to know that Gandalf's hunch about Gollum was right—but for Gollum the Quest would have failed at the last moment.

From the appendices they will get tantalizing glimpses of the First and Second Ages. The legends of these are, I understand, already written and I hope that, as soon as the publishers have seen "The Lord of the Rings" into a paperback edition, they will not keep Mr. Tolkien's growing army of fans waiting too long.

Oo, Those Awful Orcs

by Edmund Wilson

In 1937, Dr. J.R.R. Tolkien, an Oxford don, published a children's book called *The Hobbit,* which had an immense success. The hobbits are a not quite human race who inhabit an imaginary country called the Shire and who combine the characteristics of certain English animals—they live in burrows like rabbits and badgers—with the traits of English country-dwellers, ranging from rustic to tweedy. (The name seems a telescoping of rabbit and Hobbs.) They have elves, trolls and dwarfs as neighbors, and they are associated with a magician called Gandalph and a slimy water-creature called Gollum. Dr. Tolkien became interested in his fairy-tale country and has gone on from this little story to elaborate a long romance, which has appeared, under the general title, *The Lord of the Rings,* in three volumes: *The Fellowship of the Ring, The Two Towers* and *The Return of the King.* All volumes are accompanied with maps, and Dr. Tolkien, who is a philologist, professor at Merton College of English Language and Literature, has equipped the last volume with a scholarly apparatus of appendices, explaining the alphabets and grammars of the various tongues spoken by his characters, and giving full genealogies and tables of historical chronology.

Dr. Tolkien has announced that this series—the hypertrophic sequel to *The Hobbit*—is intended for adults rather than children, and it has had a resounding reception at the hands of a number of critics who are certainly grown-up in years. Mr. Richard Hughes, for example, has written of it that nothing of the kind on such a scale has been attempted since *The Faerie Queen,* and that "for width of imagination it almost beggars parallel." "It's odd, you know," says Miss Naomi Mitchison, "one takes it as seriously as Malory." And Mr. C.S. Lewis, also of Oxford, is able to top them all: "If Ariosto," he ringingly writes, "rivalled it in invention (in fact, he does not), he would still lack its heroic seriousness." Nor has America been behind. In the *Saturday Review of Literature,* a Mr. Louis J. Halle, author of a book on *Civilization and Foreign Policy,* answers as follows a lady who—"lowering," he says, "her pince-nez"—has inquired what he finds in Tolkien: "What, dear lady, does this invented world have to do with our own? You ask for its meaning—as you ask for the meaning of the *Odyssey,* of *Genesis,* of *Faust*—in a word? In a word, then, its meaning is 'heroism.' It makes our own world, once more, heroic. What higher meaning than this is to be found in any literature?"

But if one goes from these eulogies to the book itself, one is likely to be let down, astonished, baffled. The reviewer has just read the whole thing aloud to his seven-year-old daughter, who has been through *The Hobbit* countless times, beginning it again the moment she has finished, and whose interest has been held by its more prolix successors. One is puzzled to know why the author should have supposed he was writing for adults. There are, to be sure, some details that are a little unpleasant for a children's book, but except when he is being pedantic and also boring the adult reader, there is little in *The Lord of the Rings* over the head of a seven-year-old child. It is essentially a children's book—a children's book which has somehow got out of hand, since, instead of directing it at the "juvenile" market, the author has indulged himself in developing the fantasy for its own sake; and it ought to be said at this point, before emphasizing its inadequacies as literature, that Dr. Tolkien makes few claims for his fairy romance. In a statement prepared for his publishers, he has explained that he began it to amuse himself, as a philological game: "The invention of languages is the foundation. The 'stories' were made rather to provide a world for the languages than the reverse. I should have preferred to write in 'Elvish'." He has omitted, he says, in the printed book, a good deal of the philological part; "but there is a great deal of linguistic matter . . . included or mythologically expressed in the book. It is to me, anyway, largely an essay in 'linguistic esthetic,' as I sometimes say to people who ask me 'what it is all about.' . . . It is not 'about' anything but itself. Certainly it has *no* allegorical intentions, general, particular or topical, moral, religious or political." An overgrown fairy story, a philological curiosity—that is, then, what *The Lord of The Rings* really is. The pretentiousness is all on the part of Dr. Tolkien's infatuated admirers, and it is these pretensions that I would here assail.

The most distinguished of Tolkien's admirers and the most conspicuous of his defenders has been Mr. W.H. Auden. That Auden is a master of English verse and a well-equipped critic of verse, no one, as they say, will dispute. It is significant, then, that he comments on the badness of Tolkien's verse—there is a great deal of poetry in *The Lord of the Rings.* Mr. Auden is apparently quite insensitive—through lack of interest in the other department—to the fact that Tolkien's prose is just as bad. Prose and verse are on the same level of professorial amateurishness. What I believe has misled Mr. Auden is his own special preoccupation with the legendary theme of the Quest. He has written a book about the literature of the Quest; he has experimented with the theme himself in a remarkable sequence of sonnets; and it is to be hoped that he will do something with it on an even larger scale. In the meantime—as sometimes happens with works that fall in with one's interests—he no doubt so overrates *The Lord of the Rings* because he reads into it something that he means to write himself. It is indeed the tale of a Quest, but, to the reviewer, an extremely unrewarding one. The hero has no serious temptations; is lured by no insidious enchantments, perplexed by few problems. What we get is a simple confrontation—in more or less the traditional terms of British melodrama—of the Forces of Evil with the Forces of Good, the remote and alien villain

with the plucky little home-grown hero. There are streaks of imagination: the ancient tree-spirits, the Ents, with their deep eyes, twiggy beards, rumbly voices; the Elves, whose nobility and beauty is elusive and not quite human. But even these are rather clumsily handled. There is never much development in the episodes; you simply go on getting more of the same thing. Dr. Tolkien has little skill at narrative and no instinct for literary form. The characters talk a story-book language that might have come out of Howard Pyle, and as personalities they do not impose themselves. At the end of this long romance, I had still no conception of the wizard Gandalph, who is a cardinal figure, had never been able to visualize him at all. For the most part such characterizations as Dr. Tolkien is able to contrive are perfectly stereotyped: Frodo the good little Englishman, Samwise, his doglike servant, who talks lower-class and respectful, and never deserts his master. These characters who are no characters are involved in interminable adventures the poverty of invention displayed in which is, it seems to me, almost pathetic. On the country in which the Hobbits, the Elves, the Ents and the

Oliphant

other Good People live, the Forces of Evil are closing in, and they have to band together to save it. The hero is the Hobbit called Frodo who has become possessed of a ring that Sauron, the King of the Enemy, wants (that learned reptilian suggestion—doesn't it give you a goosefleshy feeling?). In spite of the author's disclaimer, the struggle for the ring does seem to have some larger significance. This ring, if one continues to carry it, confers upon one special powers, but it is felt to become heavier and heavier; it exerts on one a sinister influence that one has to brace oneself to resist. The problem is for Frodo to get rid of it before he can succumb to this influence.

Now, this situation does create interest; it does seem to have possibilities. One looks forward to a queer dilemma, a new kind of hair-breadth escape, in which Frodo, in the Enemy's kingdom, will find himself half-seduced into taking over the enemy's point of view, so that the realm of shadows and horrors will come to seem to him, once he is in it, once he is strong in the power of the ring, a plausible and pleasant place, and he will narrowly escape the danger of becoming a monster himself. But these bugaboos are not magnetic; they are feeble and rather blank; one does not feel they have any real power. The Good People simply say "Boo" to them. There are Black Riders, of whom everyone is terrified but who never seem anything but specters. There are dreadful hovering birds—think of it, horrible birds of prey! There are ogreish disgusting Orcs, who, however, rarely get to the point of committing any overt acts. There is a giant female spider—a dreadful creepy-crawly spider!—who

Orcs

lives in a dark cave and eats people. What one misses in all these terrors is any trace of concrete reality. The preternatural, to be effective, should be given some sort of solidity, a real presence, recognizable features—like Gulliver, like Gogol, like Poe; not like those phantom horrors of Algernon Blackwood which prove so disappointing after the travel-book substantiality of the landscapes in which he evokes them. Tolkien's horrors resemble these in their lack of real contact with their victims, who dispose of them as we do of the horrors in dreams by simply pushing them or puffing them away. As for Sauron, the ruler of Mordor (doesn't the very name have a shuddery sound?) who concentrates in his person everything that is threatening the Shire, the build-up for him goes on through three volumes. He makes his first, rather promising, appearance as a terrible fire-rimmed yellow eye seen in a water-mirror. But this is as far as we ever get. Once Sauron's realm is invaded, we think we are going to meet him; but he still remains nothing but a burning eye scrutinizing all that occurs from the window of a remote dark tower. This might, of course, be made effective; but actually it is not; we never feel Sauron's power. And the climax, to which we have been working up through exactly nine hundred and ninety-nine large close-printed pages, when it comes, proves extremely flat. The ring is at last got rid of by being dropped into a fiery crater, and the kingdom of Sauron "topples" in a brief and banal earthquake that sets fire to everything and burns it up, and so releases the author from the necessity of telling the reader what exactly was so terrible there. Frodo has come to the end of his Quest, but the reader has remained untouched by the wounds and fatigues of his journey. An impotence of imagination seems to me to sap the whole story. The wars are never dynamic; the ordeals give no sense of strain; the fair ladies would not stir a heartbeat; the horrors would not hurt a fly.

Now, how is it that these long-winded volumes of what looks to this reviewer like balderdash have elicited such tributes as those above? The answer is, I believe, that certain people—especially, perhaps, in Britain—have a lifelong appetite for juvenile trash. They would not accept adult trash, but, confronted with the pre-teen-age article, they revert to the mental phase which delighted in *Elsie Dinsmore* and *Little Lord Fauntleroy* and which seems to have made of Billy Bunter, in England, almost a national figure. You can see it in the tone they fall into when they talk about Tolkien in print: they bubble, they squeal, they coo; they go on about Malory and Spenser—both of whom have a charm and a distinction that Tolkien has never touched.

As for me, if we must read about imaginary kingdoms, give me James Branch Cabell's Poictesme. He at least writes for grown-up people, and he does not present the drama of life as a showdown between Good People and Goblins. He can cover more ground in an episode that lasts only three pages than Tolkien is able to in one of his twenty-page chapters and he can create a more disquieting impression by a reference to something that is never described than Tolkien through his whole demonology.

A Trip through Middle-earth:

A Chronology of <u>The Hobbit</u> and <u>The Lord of the Rings</u>

by Douglas Kendall

A newcomer to Middle-earth quickly finds himself engulfed in a vast and sometimes confusing world with a past as lengthy and diverse as our own. *The Hobbit* and *The Lord of the Rings*, taken by themselves, make up a minute but significant interval in the history of Tolkien's world. When Bilbo Baggins was surprised by the visit of Gandalf, Thorin, and the other dwarves, almost three ages of Middle-earth had passed.

The First Age, which is described in great detail in *The Silmarillion*, ended in the destruction of Morgoth, the first great Enemy. However, with the survival of his servant Sauron, the battle of good and evil continued into the Second Age, that of the glory of Númenor. Sauron managed to corrupt all but a few faithful Númenoreans, leading to King Ar-Pharazon's futile attack on Valinor. At this sacrilege, Númenor and her army were destroyed. Only Elendil the Tall and his faithful Númenoreans survived the disaster to settle in Middle-earth.

The Second Age ended in the Last Alliance of Elves and Men, and the defeat of Sauron. By this time the Rings of Power had been forged and distributed, and at the Siege of Barad-dur the Great Ring was taken from Sauron by Isildur, Elendil's son. His decision not to destroy the Ring allowed Bilbo Baggins to stumble across it in the roots of the Misty Mountains almost three thousand years later.

What was Middle-earth like when the only son of Bungo and Belladonna Baggins was born? The great kingdoms of Arnor and Gondor were only shadows of their former greatness. In the north, all that remained of Arnor was wild country interspersed with quiet districts of rural dwellers, such as the hobbits of the Shire and the men and hobbits of the Bree-land. Here and there, bands of elves roamed the land, awaiting their final voyage from the Grey Havens. In Rivendell, Elrond wielded Vilya, the most powerful of the three Elven Rings, making his valley a refuge for the free peoples as the disorder of the outside world continued to grow.

The kingdom of Gondor remained the most powerful remnant of the Númenorean men, but it had been without a king for over eight hundred years. The Riders of Rohan had first given their aid to Gondor nearly four centuries earlier, yet Gondor was still hard pressed by the men of Harad and the Corsairs of Umbar. These forces were constantly stirred to war by Sauron, who was rising again in his fortress of Barad-dur. The power of Gondor was clearly on the wane, despite the pride and heritage of her people.

In the north of Eriador, the power of Galadriel kept Lórien free from the Enemy's attacks, but to the Men of Rohan and Gondor, she seemed mysterious and dangerous. Moria lay empty, the wars of the dwarves and orcs at an end, temporarily at least. Still farther north, the Lakemen of Esgaroth coexisted with the Silvan Elves of Mirkwood, neither daring to disturb the stronghold of the dragon, Smaug, in the Lonely Mountain.

Until one late April morning in the year 2941 of the Third Age, Bilbo Baggins had been a perfectly ordinary and quite well-to-do bachelor hobbit, although his mother was of the Took family, which had a reputation for producing adventurers. On this fine spring morning, the wizard Gandalf appeared on Bilbo's doorstep, bringing back the hobbit's fond memories of fireworks put on by this ancient enchanter years before. Like most hobbits, Bilbo thought of the old man as some sort of itinerant magician, never realizing his importance in the world outside the Shire. Thinking to be rid of this increasingly bothersome visitor, Bilbo invited Gandalf to tea the following week, undoubtedly hoping the wizard would be in faraway parts by that time.

But Gandalf returned, accompanied by thirteen dwarves, led by Thorin Oakenshield, heir to Erebor, the Kingdom under the Mountain in Wilderland. As Bilbo's unexpectedly large tea party progressed, he discovered to his horror that he was being included in Thorin's quest to regain his kingdom—not to mention his treasure—from the dragon, Smaug.

The next morning, awaking to find no Gandalf and no dwarves, Bilbo was inclined to believe that Thorin and Company had left without him. However, the wizard soon appeared, bidding him to be off and directing him to hurry to the Green Dragon in Bywater. Thus Mr. Bilbo Baggins was sent off on his great adventure without so much as a pocket handkerchief on his person.

The expedition traveled east along the Great Road, but the first event of interest didn't occur until May 30 (or Thrimidge 30, in Shire Reckoning). It was a rainy day, and the travelers were between Weathertop and the Ford of Bruinen, to the north of the road, when

the dwarves risked approaching a campfire in the wild. Or rather, they sent their companion first—and Bilbo was caught picking a troll's pocket! The dwarves were soon captured too when they tried to discover what had become of their hobbit friend. Luckily Gandalf tricked the three trolls into staying outside until dawn, and, as everyone knows, trolls turn to stone by the light of day. So Bilbo and his friends were rescued from their first snare.

By early June, the company had reached Rivendell, the hidden valley of Elrond Half-elven, one of the great amongst the Eldar of Middle-earth. Here Thorin and Gandalf discovered the directions to a secret entrance into the Lonely Mountain, written in moon-letters on an old map. After about a fortnight of rest and relaxation

Shadowfax

amongst the people of Elrond, Thorin and his band departed to attempt the crossing of the great Misty Mountains.

One Monday evening, after they had left Rivendell far behind, the incident that made Bilbo's adventure truly extraordinary began to unfold. In a mountain pass, the expedition was ambushed and captured by a band of orcs, or goblins. Taken underground into the Chamber of the Great Goblin, Bilbo and the dwarves had another narrow escape. This time Gandalf rescued them amidst lightning and explosions, which killed the Great Goblin.

Pursued by furious orcs, Gandalf led the company toward an exit from beneath the mountains. But the orcs managed to overtake the fleeing dwarves and in the ensuing struggle Bilbo hit his head on a rock and rolled out of the way. There he remained for some time. Finally, he awoke and found himself quite alone. Following a tunnel for some distance, Bilbo reached a dead end: a cold, dank, underground lake, from which there soon emerged a wiry, slimy creature with large, pale eyes. This was Gollum, who for ages had feasted on orcs and any other creatures who happened to stray near his pool. Furthermore, his natural cunning was supplemented by his ownership of a magic ring which rendered him invisible. As luck would have it (or was it luck?), this was exactly the ring which Bilbo, seemingly by accident, had slipped into his pocket on regaining consciousness.

If Gollum had had his ring with him, he would have made short work of our hobbit friend. As it was, he had to stall for time, so he challenged Bilbo to a riddle game. If Bilbo won, Gollum agreed to show his opponent the way out of the mountain. If Gollum was the victor, he would feast on hobbit.

After several rounds, Bilbo could think of no further riddles and, in desperation, asked Gollum to guess what was in his pocket. Gollum thought this hardly fair, and returned to his island to put on his ring and finish off his prey. When he discovered that it was missing, Gollum guessed the riddle's answer too late. The ring slid onto Bilbo's finger almost voluntarily, and Gollum found no hobbit waiting for his return. Invisible, Bilbo made his way out of the mountains and astounded the dwarves by appearing again in their midst. It was now Thursday; the ambush of the orcs had occurred on Monday night.

The company was not so easily rid of the danger of these enemies. As they travelled down out of the mountains and Thursday evening fell, a party of orcs and wargs surrounded them, forcing them up into trees and setting the trees afire. This time, it was not Gandalf who engineered the escape but the Lord of the Eagles of Middle-earth, Gwaihir. Through sheer good fortune he had noticed the plight of Thorin's band as he circled far above the earth. A hater of orcs and wargs, he was quick to rescue the treed dwarves, wizard, and hobbit. While the eagles play more important roles later on in *The Hobbit* and also in *The Lord of the Rings,* at this point they simply set the grateful company down the next morning on a rock in the middle of the Anduin, or Great River, of Wilderland.

On Friday, Gandalf led the party to the home of Beorn, a most extraordinary man who could change his body into that of a bear. He was quite impressive even in his human form. After Gandalf, Thorin, and the others had been accepted as Beorn's guests, the wizard warned his friends not to leave the house at night, for this was the time when Beorn prowled outdoors and was capable of killing any of them easily. They followed his advice and lived to hear Beorn's warnings about the perils of Mirkwood, the vast forest they would have to cross in order to reach the Lonely Mountain. Mirkwood was full of unknown perils, as the company would soon find out.

Four days' ride from Beorn's house the company reached the

entrance to the forest. There, Bilbo and the dwarves were alarmed when they discovered that Gandalf would not be accompanying them on this dangerous part of the journey. The wizard had other affairs to tend to which, as it turned out, consisted of repelling the newly rising shadow of Sauron from his stronghold in Southern Mirkwood, Dol Guldur. But the dwarves and Bilbo weren't much concerned with that; their own predicament was more than enough to think about.

Once in the forest, the travelers lost track of time. Each day seemed equally dark and gloomy, each night pitch dark and full of watching eyes. Then the first of several disasters occurred. In crossing an enchanted river, Bombur, the fattest of the dwarves, fell into the water. Under its spell, he immediately fell sound asleep, presenting a rather heavy burden for the rest of the party to carry.

In addition, the woods now rang continually with eerie laughter, and soon came the sounds of a great hunt off to the north of their path. As their food ran out, the travelers were lured off the path—the one thing above all that Beorn had warned against—by the sights, sounds, and smells of a great woodland feast. Yet each time the companions entered the circle of the feast, the fires were doused and the elvish people (for such they were) melted into the shadows, leading Bilbo and the dwarves further astray each time. The exhausted company would have made easy prey for the giant spiders of Mirkwood if not for some quick thinking on the part of Bilbo. Slipping on his ring, he managed to taunt the spiders into chasing his invisible voice, leading them away from the dwarves, who were drugged and hanging in a very large spider's web. Finally, with the aid of his elvish sword Sting, Bilbo managed to rescue his friends and lead them back to the remains of one of the elvish fire rings they had seen two nights before. But when they arrived, they discovered to their horror that Thorin himself was missing.

Thorin was where they all would soon be—in the dungeon of the king of the Wood-elves. He had been captured before the spiders had come on the scene, and the suspicious King had been questioning him ever since. The day after the battle with the spiders, the elves caught up with the rest of the company, and easily rounded up the exhausted dwarves. Luckily, Bilbo managed to slip on his ring and escape. This time Bilbo freed his friends by packing them into empty wine barrels and floating them down the Forest River to Esgaroth, a town on the Long Lake. The date was September 22, Bilbo's fifty-first birthday.

In Esgaroth, Thorin's band was met enthusiastically by the inhabitants, who seemed to expect torrents of gold to come their way immediately. But the master of the town was more cautious and probably felt relieved when the expedition left Lake-town for the mountain in late autumn. In four days they had reached the Desolation of the Dragon and camped on the slopes of Erebor, the Lonely Mountain. Yet their adventures had only begun.

In the last week of autumn, they discovered the secret door described in the moon-letters of Thrór's map. This paved the way for Bilbo's part of the expedition to begin in earnest. On the same day, the hobbit (wearing his invisible ring, of course) entered the Cave of Smaug and conversed with the dragon. Unfortunately, Bilbo let the location of his secret tunnel slip, and Smaug flew out to try to catch the dwarves by surprise. The party's ponies fell victim to the fire of the dragon, but Bilbo managed to herd the dwarves into the safety of the tunnel.

The next day Bilbo returned to Smaug's lair. This time his mention of the term "Barrel-rider" infuriated Smaug, who flew off to destroy Lake-town. Though he did set the town afire, the sharp eye of Bard the Bowman spied the single weak spot in Smaug's armor. His arrow found its mark, and Smaug fell to his death in the Long Lake.

But the dwarves were not to regain their treasure so easily. The wood-elves and the Lake-men expected their share, and sent armies to back up their demands. Despite the unfavorable numbers, Thorin stubbornly refused to divide up his new wealth, and the dwarves were reinforced by their kinsmen from the Iron Hills. A major battle between the elves and men on one side and the dwarves on the other appeared imminent when Gandalf came to warn of a greater disaster at hand: an army of orcs was bearing down on them all.

This battle raged for hours, and during the fighting Bilbo tried as much as possible to stay invisible. Despite heroics on all sides, Thorin was mortally injured, and it took the intervention of the eagles and Beorn (in his bear shape) to defeat the orcs. At last, the quest was over—or so it seemed. Thorin was buried under the mountain, and his kinsman Dain rebuilt the kingdom of Erebor. Bard became king of Dale, and Bilbo slowly made his way back to Hobbiton. He spent the yuletide with Beorn, arrived at Rivendell once again on May 1, and finally trudged up the path to Bag End on June 22, 2942, only to find his possessions about to be put up for auction by his greedy relatives, the Sackville-Bagginses. After all this was straightened out and he was finally settled in, Bilbo developed a reputation as one of the Shire's most wealthy and eccentric citizens. Yet the greatest treasure Bilbo brought home with him was kept secret. Later he would realize the ring's importance, but for the moment, it appeared that hobbit adventures were over.

The years between Bilbo's return from Erebor and the events described in *The Lord of the Rings* were years of cautious but open expansion by Sauron and slow but continual decay on the part of his opponents. Just ten years after Thorin's quest, the Black Lord declared himself openly and set out to rebuild his great fortress of Barad-dur. He also sent his agents, the Nazgul, to reoccupy his former stronghold, Dol Guldur in Mirkwood, from which he had been driven the year of Bilbo's adventures.

At the same time, cracks were beginning to show in the ranks of Sauron's foes. The White Council, an organization of the Eldar (elven lords) and the Istari (wizards), had been watching for the reappearance of the Great Enemy for years. The Council included both Gandalf and Elrond, but its leader was the most powerful of

Guard of Minas Tirith

the wizards, Saruman the White. Saruman had made the study of the Rings of Power his specialty, and after many years he came to desire possession of the One Ring himself. He made no sign of this to his fellow council members, but quietly watched for the discovery of the lost Ring. In 2953, the White Council met for the last time. Here Saruman reported that the Ring had been washed to sea, lost forever. Meanwhile he fortified his dwelling place at Isengard and accelerated his own search for the Ring.

Gandalf was next in power to Saruman, so he attracted the traitor's jealousy and fear. All his movements were watched by Saruman's spies. In the years that followed, Gandalf kept a lively interest in hobbits in general and Bilbo in particular, for he had always doubted Bilbo's tale of winning his ring as a prize. Thus Saruman's attention was also attracted to the Shire.

By now Saruman had been overcome by his own lust for the Ring. Daring to look into one of the Seeing Stones of Gondor (the *palantíri*), he was ensnared by the more powerful will of Sauron, who also possessed one of the stones. It was in this way that the Dark Lord probably first heard of the Shire. Gandalf, in turn, began to fear for the safety of the Shire, and so he persuaded the Rangers of Arnor, descendants of the kings, to keep watch over the borders. The chief of these Rangers, Aragorn, was the heir to the thrones of both Gondor and Arnor, and had become a close friend of Gandalf.

This then was where events stood in 3001, at the opening of *The Lord of the Rings.* Bilbo was nearing his eleventy-first birthday, and his nephew Frodo would be thirty-three (his coming of age) on the same day. To celebrate this momentous occasion, the old hobbit planned the greatest party the Shire had ever seen. After his return from the wild, his neighbors had always considered Bilbo somewhat eccentric, but this time he outdid himself. He called on many helpers—including the dwarves and Gandalf—to plan a party that featured fireworks and food the likes of which had never been imagined before in Hobbiton. And at the close of the required thank-you speech, Bilbo simply disappeared, slipping on his ring in a cloud of smoke provided by Gandalf.

Aside from astounding his many guests, Bilbo seriously worried the wizard, who had long suspected that the hobbit's ring was in fact the One Ring. He persuaded Bilbo to leave the ring with Frodo when he departed for "retirement" in Rivendell, and Bilbo agreed very reluctantly. The ring had become an enormous burden on Bilbo's mind, and now this burden was passing to Frodo.

For some time, all seemed well. Gandalf visited the Shire at various times, and there seemed no cause for alarm. But after 3008, Gandalf's visits ceased for over nine years. When he returned, on the twelfth of April, 3018, he was ready to divulge to Frodo the truth he had learned: Frodo's ring and the One Ring sought for so many years by Sauron were one and the same. The Ring had to be destroyed if Sauron were to be utterly defeated, yet that meant a dangerous journey to the heart of Mordor to hurl the Ring into the Cracks of Doom. As if this wasn't difficult enough, Gandalf warned Frodo that the Ring also acquired power over its possessor. Even if he managed to reach Mount Doom, the Ring-bearer would face a great internal struggle when the time came to toss the Ring away.

From this point forward, the pace of events quickened considerably. Gandalf left, advising Frodo to depart for Rivendell no later than his birthday, with his friend Sam Gamgee accompanying him.

In June Sauron launched an attack on Osgiliath, the former capital of Gondor. Sauron was planning a much mightier offensive, but even this first foray made obvious the overwhelming odds against Gondor. In July, Boromir, the son of the Steward of Gondor, departed his own land to seek the semilegendary Imladris (Rivendell) to seek the advice of Elrond. Meanwhile the creature Gollum had escaped captivity in the Forest of Mirkwood, setting off in search of Baggins, the "thief" who had stolen his ring.

Also in July, Gandalf fell into the hands of Saruman, who tried at first to convince his colleague to join in his treachery, and then imprisoned him on the pinnacle of his tower, Orthanc. It wasn't until mid-September that Gandalf escaped, carried from the tower by the Lord of the Eagles. The wizard then spent several days taming a horse he had gotten from the Riders of Rohan. By the time the fleet Shadowfax obeyed Gandalf's command, September 22, the day he was to have met Frodo, had passed.

On September 23 Frodo finally left Bag End for Crickhollow in Buckland. By this time, though, the Black Riders of Sauron, wraiths under the power of the Black Lord, had entered the Shire. Any further delay on Frodo's part would have meant the end of the journey before its beginning. As it was, Frodo and his companions had several near brushes with a Rider before arriving in Buckland.

Gandalf was hurrying to the Shire, but by September 26 Frodo, accompanied by Sam Gamgee, Merry Brandybuck, and Pippin Took, had plunged into the Old Forest, eluding the Black Riders but also becoming hopelessly lost themselves. Luckily they were rescued by an ancient manlike creature of the forest, Tom Bombadil, with whom they spent two nights. After being captured by a barrow-wight, and being rescued once again by Bombadil, the hobbits arrived at the village of Bree on September 29, even as Gandalf arrived in Hobbiton.

The night at Bree brought both good and bad fortune to the company. They reluctantly took up with a Ranger called Strider, who proved to be Gandalf's friend Aragorn, their guide to Rivendell. However, in a drunken singing bout, Frodo committed the gaffe of using the Ring and disappearing before a tavernful of people—just after Pippin had described Bilbo's farewell feast! With spies abroad, it was not surprising that the inn at Bree was raided by Black Riders that same night, as was the house in Buckland.

With Strider's help, the hobbits avoided meeting the Black Riders once again, and they left Bree with their guide early the next day. By nightfall Gandalf had reached Bree. The next morning, October 1, he galloped off along the Great East Road, actually overtaking the hobbits, who were struggling through marshes and rough country to the north of the Road. When the company reached the strategic hill of Weathertop, they found evidence of a great fire. This had, in fact, been caused by a clash between Gandalf and the Black Riders three nights earlier. At Weathertop, Frodo was gravely wounded in an attack by the Riders.

Strider continued to lead the company through the rough terrain, aiming for the Bridge of Mitheithel. When they crossed it, on September 13, they found a token left by the great elven lord Glorfindel, sent by Elrond to find the Ring-bearer. But it was not until five days later that they met—the same day on which Gandalf reached Rivendell. Two days later, the company met the Black Riders at the Ford of Bruinen, but the wraiths were swept away in a flood contrived by Gandalf. Thus Frodo reached Rivendell safely and began his recovery. By September 24, the date of Boromir's arrival at Rivendell, Frodo had regained consciousness.

The next day, Elrond opened a great council of the free peoples, called to discuss their predicament. During this meeting, Frodo agreed to seek the destruction of the Ring and was given several companions to aid him in this quest: Sam, Merry, Pippin, Gandalf, Strider (Aragorn), Boromir, the Wood-elf Legolas, and the dwarf Gimli (the son of Gloin, who had been one of Bilbo's companions on his earlier journey). Two months of relative peace in Rivendell followed before the Fellowship of the Ring departed on December 25.

A scant three weeks later, Frodo and his companions had already begun to run into trouble. In the desolate land of Eregion they were spied upon by evil-looking birds, and as they attempted to cross the Misty Mountains through the Redhorn Pass, they were buffeted by extraordinary blizzards and forced to turn back. It was clear that someone did not want the group to traverse the mountains by that path. The only alternative was the treacherous journey through the Mines of Moria, formerly the greatest of the dwarves' strongholds, but now deserted and eerie after the wars of the orcs and dwarves.

Withstanding an attack by wolves, Gandalf led the company into the mines on January 13. Although they emerged on the eastern side only two days later, their time within the mountains had seemed like an eternity. First of all, Frodo sensed that someone had picked up their trail and was following them—Gollum had been in the mines and naturally was attracted to the Ring-bearer. Second, the travelers discovered that a dwarf colony founded only five years earlier by Balin had been destroyed, not only by orcs but also by some nameless terror. Finally, on January 15, the company found themselves in the same position: trapped by orcs, they had to fight their way to the east entrance of the mines. There they discovered what had terrorized Balin's colony: a balrog, a creature of the Elder Days possessing great power of both shadow and fire. It took all of Gandalf's powers to hold off the monster while his friends escaped over the bridge to relative safety. Then Gandalf broke the bridge, sending both himself and the balrog tumbling into the abyss. The fellowship was safe, but it had lost its most powerful member. As Aragorn led the remaining companions out of Moria, all hearts were downcast.

While the fellowship reached the forest of Lórien, home of the great elven queen Galadriel on January 17, Gandalf's ordeal continued. He battled the balrog as they fell, then pursued him to the peak of Zirak-zigil, from which he cast the balrog down on January 25. Gandalf the Grey passed away at this time, but the wizard's story had not truly ended. By the time the fellowship left Lórien on February 16, Gandalf the White had returned to life. Once again, Gwaihir the eagle bore Gandalf to safety, this time to Galadriel's realm.

But Frodo, Aragorn, and their company knew nothing of this turn of events as they continued by boat down the Anduin River. By this time, it was certain that Gollum was still following, floating along by log. It was also apparent that the company had to choose its path: toward Mordor to destroy the Ring, or toward Minas Tirith, first city of Gondor. There the Ring would be kept unused as long as the gates could withstand the Enemy's onslaught, or it could be used against Sauron. On February 25, the company camped at Parth Galen, just above Rauros Falls. A decision had to be made.

The choice would be Frodo's, but Boromir was so anxious that the Ring should go to his own city that he disturbed the hobbit's meditation. Indeed, he so frightened Frodo that Ring-bearer chose to use his Ring and disappear. As the fellowship searched for Frodo, they made easy targets for an orc raid, and Boromir was killed defending Merry and Pippin, who were taken alive for questioning by Saruman. Frodo, now convinced that he must dispose of the Ring on himself, tried to slip away to the east side of the river without attracting any attention, but the faithful Sam noticed in time. So, as Frodo set out on the last leg of his quest, he was not alone.

But the fellowship was splintered beyond repair. Gandalf had fallen, Boromir was dead, Frodo and Sam had set out for the heart of Mordor. Meanwhile Merry and Pippin were captives of the orc band and Aragorn, Legolas, and Gimli were striving to remain on the trail of the two young hobbits. This was February 26. The action recorded in the second book of the trilogy, *The Two Towers,* took place in under a month, as the tales of the scattered members of the fellowship were recorded.

Though subjected to the harsh treatment to be expected from orcs, Merry and Pippin were too valuable to be seriously damaged. Thus they managed to survive until an opportunity for escape presented itself in Fangorn Forest on February 29. The orcs had been overtaken by the cavalry of Éomer, a lord of Rohan. In the ensuing battle, the orcs were routed, and the hobbits slipped into the forest. There they met a very unusual friend, Treebeard the ent, one of that race of tree-herds. Ents are patient and thoughtful in the extreme, but the appearance of Merry and Pippin seemed to rouse Treebeard and his people from mere brooding over the behavior of Saruman's orcs to action against the wizard. After a three-day entmoot, Treebeard led a march against Isengard on March 2. With their tremendous treelike strength, the Ents had largely destroyed Saruman's compound by the next day.

While all this was happening, Aragorn and his companions had continued their search. Meeting Éomer, they heard of the destruction of the orcs, but naturally learned nothing of the hobbits since they had slipped off unnoticed. Scouring the caves of Fangorn Forest, the three searchers met a mysterious old man dressed in white. They were sure he was up to no good—and suspected he might even be Saruman himself. But on a second meeting, Aragorn recognized Gandalf, and the old friends were reunited. Thus on the same day that the ents attacked Isengard, Gandalf and Aragorn, along with Gimli and Legolas, arrived at Edoras, the royal seat of Rohan. Here Gandalf rescued King Théoden from the evil counsels of Gríma Wormtongue, who had been the king's most trusted advisor, as well as an agent of Saruman.

The following day, Aragorn, Legolas, and Gimli lent their strength to the host of Rohan in a great battle with Saruman's forces in the stronghold of Helm's Deep. Although the fighting was fierce, the Rohirrim prevailed, and the surviving orcs were destroyed by the ents. Théoden and Gandalf led a parley with Saruman, whose vocal powers were still considerable. But Gandalf the White was now the greater of the two; he broke Saruman's staff and cast him out of the order of wizards. Saruman was left amid the ruins of Isengard, watched by Treebeard and the ents, while the Rohirrim began their plans to aid Gondor.

First, however, Wormtongue hurled Saruman's *palantír* out a window, missing his master but answering many of Gandalf's questions. The communication between Isengard and Mordor was revealed, and the peril of the West made more clear. By night, Pippin Took dared to gaze into the Seeing-stone. Perceived by Sauron, his mind was probed by the Dark Lord, but luckily he survived unharmed. Gandalf now decided to ride ahead to Gondor, with Pippin, first delivering the *palantír* to Aragorn, its rightful owner. So as Gandalf and Pippin galloped south on March 5, the scene shifted to Frodo's journey.

Although Frodo had managed to give his companions the slip, within a few days he and Sam discovered that Gollum had remained on their trail. In shadowing the Ring-bearer, the creature showed the cunning he had acquired in his youth along the Anduin River and in the roots of the Misty Mountains. But as Frodo and his pursuer descended from the rough country of the Emyn Muil, (the same day that Merry and Pippin met Treebeard in Fangorn), Gollum misstepped and was captured by the hobbits. Sam, ever practical, was in favor of killing Gollum then and there, but Frodo was moved to pity the wretched creature. After all, the Ring was having its effect on Frodo, as it had on Bilbo. Gollum (or Sméagol, as he had originally been named) had held the Ring for a much longer time and he had very nearly been consumed by its power.

Besides, Gollum had already been to Mordor and could prove an indispensable guide, if carefully guarded. So on the first day of March, Sméagol/Gollum began to pick a path across the Dead Marshes, where images of long-dead warriors terrified the travelers. By the time Gandalf and King Théoden had parleyed with Saruman, Frodo had reached the northern gate to Mordor. Finding this entrance impassable, Frodo was forced to trust Sméagol, who promised to guide them to a hidden pathway into Sauron's land. So at dusk on March 5, Frodo turned south, toward the empty land of Ithilien. Gandalf was even then hurrying toward the desperate city of Minas Tirith.

The following day, Aragorn was joined by his kinsmen, the Rangers of Arnor. Having revealed himself through the *palantír* to Sauron, and having wrestled in thought with the Dark Lord, Aragorn was urged by the sons of Elrond to use the Paths of the Dead to reach Gondor quickly. This was a grim mountain path from Dunharrow (where Théoden prepared for his march to Minas Tirith) to the Stone of Erech. To the distress of all the Rohirrim, and especially Éowyn, the king's niece, Aragorn chose this path from which none had returned.

Meanwhile Frodo had fallen in with a company of soldiers of Gondor who were patrolling the borders of Mordor. Their leader was Faramir, brother of Boromir. Being reasonably learned in lore

Revenge of the Rohirrim

and a friend of Gandalf's, he easily guessed Frodo's mission. Faramir resisted the temptation to take the Ring and use it to defend his city. Instead, he sent the hobbits on their way after warning them not to trust Gollum's secret path.

The next day, March 9, was an eventful one for all the scattered companions. Gandalf and Pippin succeeded in reaching Minas Tirith before the city was besieged by the armies of Mordor. Here Pippin became a knight of Gondor under the Steward Denethor, a ruler embittered at the loss of one son (Boromir) and the supposed unfaithfulness of another (Faramir).

Aragorn and the Rangers, along with Legolas and Gimli, survived the passage to Erech, where Aragorn summoned an enormous host of the dead to follow him. These shades had broken their oaths to Isildur centuries earlier and had been condemned to unrest until the heir of Elendil called on them. The ghostly army scattered most of the terrified folk of Gondor before them, but some hardy men joined Aragorn's host.

As Frodo reached the road to the corrupt city of Minas Morgul, a great darkness issued forth from Mordor, a darkness which would cover all the lands east of the Misty Mountains. The next day, Frodo and Sam witnessed the marching of a great Morgul host toward Gondor. The war had finally begun in earnest.

On March 10, the army of Rohan also set forth toward Gondor; by now one army already stood in their path to Minas Tirith. Aragorn was marching north with the dead, but the siege of the city was already being prepared.

Meanwhile, Frodo was rejoined by Gollum, who was ready to lead the hobbits along the secret way—straight to the lair of a monstrous spider, Shelob. Once in the trap, Frodo was poisoned by the spider. Thinking that his master was dead, a distraught Sam took the Ring and prepared to continue the journey alone. But just as he was about to leave the motionless body of his master, a party of orcs appeared. Discovering that Frodo had merely been drugged by the spider (who had in turn been grievously wounded by the enraged Sam), the orcs dragged the body off to their guard tower. Sam followed close behind.

By this time Aragorn had routed the Black Lord's fleet through the terror of the Dead, and sailed up the Anduin toward the city. But in the meantime the Pelennor Fields outside the walls had been over-run, and Faramir had been grievously wounded by a Nazgul. Théoden and his forces were in Druadan Forest planning a maneuver that would get them past the first orc army without having to face a full battle.

The following day, Sam found Frodo in the Tower of Cirith Ungol. He also discovered that two opposing orc factions in the tower's guard had conveniently killed each other off. This helped the pair to return to their quest by the next day, although Frodo had lost Sting, as well as his elven cloak and dwarvish mail shirt during his captivity.

Minas Tirith was by now under full siege. Théoden, with the aid of the Wild Men of Druadan, had avoided battle with the army arrayed to stop him. But early on March 15, the Chief of the Nazgul, the Witch King, managed to break the gates of the city. Denethor, despairing at this turn of events and crazed from gazing into his *palantír,* burned himself on a pyre. Only the disobedience of the guard Beregond saved an unconscious Faramir from the same fate.

As the cock crowed, Théoden led the Rohirrim into battle with the besiegers and the Battle of the Pelennor Fields began. The tide turned first to one side, then the other. The arrival of Aragorn helped defeat the forces of Sauron, but the victory of Gondor was only sealed when the Witch King was killed. Having just slain Théoden, the Nazgul was stabbed by Merry Brandybuck and Éowyn, who had been disguised as a warrior. The Witch king, it had been told, would not perish by the hand of man, and so it was that he fell to the swords of a hobbit and a woman.

Though Minas Tirith was saved, the plight of Gondor remained desperate, for Sauron still had vast armies of Easterlings and Southrons, as well as orcs, at his disposal. And the armies of Gondor and her allies had suffered great losses.

But the king had returned to Gondor. Aragorn had raised the standard of Elendil and his healing touch had been witnessed on the wounded. And although he would not yet take up his throne, nonetheless the rumor of the king's return was a fresh hope to the citizens. So on March 18, the Host of the West, led by Aragorn and Gandalf the White, marched forth to give battle to Sauron one last, decisive time.

In the far north of Eriador, the wood-elves of Mirkwood had repelled an attack from Dol Gulduron the same day that the siege of

Minas Tirith was lifted. Two days later, Sauron's northern army attacked Dale, and both men and dwarves were forced to take refuge in Erebor, which was well suited to withstand a siege. Both King Brand of Dale and King Dain of the Mountain fell in battle in Dale. In Lórien, the elves withstood three assaults of the enemy, so far was Sauron's power extended in those days.

Inside Mordor, Frodo and Sam continued their difficult journey. On March 18, the hobbits fell in with a band of orcs marching north toward the great gate of Sauron's land. Only the orc-garb they wore kept them from capture, and they managed to escape the following day. Next they turned along the road to Sauron's citadel of Barad-dur, just as the Host of the West reached the Vale of Minas Morgul.

As Aragorn marched through Ithilien toward Cirith Gorgor, the gate of Mordor, Frodo and Sam left the road to trudge across the rough country to Mount Doom. The following day, March 23, the hobbits discarded their gear in the arid waste of Mordor, even as Aragorn was dismissing the faint-hearted among his followers.

The army halted, at last, one day later, before the great Towers of the Teeth which guarded the entrance to Sauron's land. Here they parleyed with a grim messenger known as the Mouth of Sauron, who demanded the surrender of the captains and displayed Frodo's captured armor. This stole all hope from Sauron's opponents, leaving only a grim determination to fight to the death. So the battle began, as hordes of orcs, trolls, and men of the East and the South set upon the surrounded army of Gondor.

But of course Frodo had not been captured. He had indeed made his way to the Sammath Naur, the Chambers of Fire that held the Cracks of Doom. But now he felt the power of the Ring at its greatest. He could not throw it into the fire. Instead, he raised it on his finger, claiming it as his own. At this moment, Sauron perceived him and hurriedly called the Nazgul to Mount Doom. Even this close to utter defeat, the Dark Lord could have retaken his Ring and had the victory, but for the unquenchable thirst of Gollum for his lost possession. Having followed Frodo to the mountain, the creature leapt at the invisible but weakened hobbit, finally taking both the Ring and the finger from his hand. Gloating insanely over his prize, Gollum stepped too far, falling into the abyss and saving the quest that had been so near to ruin.

The destruction of the Ring shook the mountain with great tremors; the volcano erupted in flame, and lava poured down its sides. Before Cirith Gorgor, the servants of Sauron fled, their driving force gone. But the Host of the West felt a new hope surge in their hearts. For even as the eagles of the North joined the fray, the Nazgul turned and fled at their master's last desperate call. The Black Gate crumbled before them, as did the Tower of Barad-dur many leagues away.

At this, Gandalf went with Gwaihir the Windlord and his kinsfolk and plucked Frodo and Sam from the ruin of Mount Doom. So the quest had succeeded and the realm of Sauron ended,

on March 25, just over six months after Frodo's hasty departure from the Shire.

The months that followed were filled with both celebration and mourning. Rohan and Gondor had lost their rulers and many brave folk, but the shadow of Mordor was gone and the king had returned at last. Aragorn was crowned Elessar Telcontar, King of Gondor and Arnor on May 1. On Mid-year's Day, he took Arwen Evenstar, the daughter of Elrond, as his queen. Their rule was to be long and peaceful.

Returning home, the four traveling hobbits found the hand of evil at work in their beloved Shire. Saruman had long maintained agents in that country and, in his bitterness, he had set about the destruction of Frodo's homeland after his own downfall. So it was that the last battle of the War of the Ring was fought at Bywater in the Shire, as the returned travelers led their people to a complete victory over the wizard's henchmen. Thus November 3 became one of the chief dates in hobbit history, the anniversary of the second and last battle fought on Shire soil; the first had been the Battle of Greenfields way back in 1147 by Shire Reckoning.

With the passing of the One Ring, the Third Age drew to a close. In the Shire, Sam supervised the restoration of the land to its former state, even adding to the beauty of the countryside with elvish gifts. But the days of the Eldar themselves in Middle-earth were growing few. After going on for many centuries, their return to Valinor was coming to its end. The mission of the wizards, to guard the free peoples against Sauron's domination, was completed. Therefore, Elrond, Galadriel, Gandalf, and a great host of elves rode west to the Grey Havens in September of T.A. 3021. In the woods of the Shire, Frodo joined them; Bilbo was already in their number. The Ring-bearers were to pass across the sea to Valinor as a reward for their deeds in Middle-earth. It was said that many years later, Sam Gamgee was also allowed this privilege, for he had been a Ring-bearer too, if only for a short time.

With the departure of this company for the Utmost West, a new age was reckoned to have begun in Middle-earth. It would be an age dominated by men. For many years the dwarves, the hobbits, and the few remaining elves maintained contact with their neighbors, but gradually they faded into legends and bedtime stories of mankind.

The Defeat of the Nazgul Chieftain

Tree by Tolkien

by Colin Wilson

A few years ago, I went to have lunch with W.H. Auden in his New York apartment. It was the first time I'd met him, and Norman Mailer had warned me that I might find him difficult to get along with. "Very reserved, very English—but more so than most Englishmen"; I found this true on the whole—he seemed to be very formal, perhaps basically shy. But after we had been eating for ten minutes, he asked me suddenly: "Do you like *The Lord of the Rings*?" I said I thought it was a masterpiece. Auden smiled, "I somehow thought you would." The manner softened noticeably, and the lunch proceeded in a more relaxed atmosphere.

It is true, as Peter S. Beagle remarked in his introduction to *The Tolkien Reader,* that Tolkien admirers form a sort of club. Donald Swann is another member—but that is understandable, for his temperament is romantic and imaginative. It is harder to understand why someone as "intellectual" as Auden should love Tolkien, while other highly intelligent people find him somehow revolting. (When I mentioned to a widely read friend—who is also an excellent critic—that I intended to write an essay on Tolkien, he said: "Good, it's time somebody really exploded that bubble," taking it completely for granted that it would be an attack.) Angus Wilson told me in 1956 that he thought *The Lord of the Rings* was "don's whimsy" (although he may have changed his mind since then).

I first tried to read the book in about 1954, when only two volumes were out. I already knew a number of people who raved about Tolkien, but who seemed unable to explain precisely why they thought him so significant. I tried the first twenty pages of Volume One, decided this was too much like Enid Blyton, and gave it up for another ten years. In the early sixties, I started to work on a book about imaginative literature, triggered by the discovery of H.P. Lovecraft; John Comley, a psychologist friend (who had himself published a couple of good novels) asked me if I didn't intend to include Tolkien in the book. I said: "I thought he was pretty dreadful?" "He's *very* good." So I bought the three volume edition of *The Lord of the Rings,* and started to read it in bed one morning. The absurd result was that I stayed in bed for three days, and read straight through it. What so impressed me on that first reading was the self-containedness of Tolkien's world. I suppose there *are* a few novelists who have created worlds that are uniquely their own— Faulkner, for example, or Dickens. But since their world is fairly close to the actual world, it cannot really be called a unique *creation.* The only parallel that occurs to me is the Wagner Ring cycle, that one can only enter as if taking a holiday on a strange planet.

I have read the book through a couple of times since—once aloud to my children. On re-reading, one notices the sentimentality. I could really do with less of Tom Bombadil, and Gimli's endless talk about the Lady of Lothlorien; but it hardly detracts from the total achievement. But on the second reading, I also noticed how Tolkien achieves the basic effect of the book—by slipping in, rather quietly, passages of "fine writing." Not really "purple passages" in the manner of some of the Victorians. They are too unobtrusive for that. I suppose what comes over most clearly from all this is that Tolkien *enjoys* creating a scene, revelling in it. This is certainly the basic strength and charm of the book.

I find it interesting to recall those comments on Tolkien, made by friends in the early fifties—precisely because they *couldn't* explain why they thought him "important." They certainly *felt* him important, something more than a writer of fantasy or fairy tales. It is also significant that there has been so little written about him, in spite of his appeal to "intellectuals." This makes it an interesting challenge—to define the exact nature and extent of Tolkien's importance.

One might begin by considering Wilson's essay, "Oo, Those Awful Orcs," for Wilson is a good critic, who leans over backwards to try to understand why anyone should admire *The Lord of the Rings.* What Wilson says, basically, is that the book is "essentially a children's book—a children's book which has somehow got out of hand, since, instead of directing it at the juvenile market, the author has indulged himself in developing fantasy for its own sake." He ends by accounting for the popularity of the book by remarking that many people, especially in Britain, have a lifelong appetite for juvenile trash.

Fortunately, Tolkien's output has not been immense— fortunately for the critic, I mean. So it is not quite as difficult as it might be to trace the development of his characteristic ideas.

Tolkien was born in 1892—an interesting fact in itself. It means that by the time he was ten years old—the age at which children begin to find their own way in literature—he was living in the middle of a literary era of great vitality and complexity. The best-sellers of the day were Kipling, Rider Haggard, Conan Doyle, Maurice Hewlett and Anthony Hope—all romantics, all influenced by Stevenson. But new figures were emerging, equally romantic, but also intellectuals—Wells, Shaw, Chesterton, and Belloc. We now tend to be dismissive about this era, thinking of it as a kind of inferior Victorian twilight, bearing the same relation to the real thing that Richard Strauss's music bears to Wagner. This is unfair and inaccurate. We are now living in an age of literary exhaustion; we get used to the bleak landscape. Cyril Connolly said that the writer's business is to produce masterpieces; but what masterpieces have been produced in the past fifty years? *Ulysses, The Waste Land,* Musil's *Man Without Qualities;* a few people would include Kafka, perhaps E. M. Forster, Hermann Broch's *Sleepwalkers,* Mann's *Magic Mountain.* And what more recently? We have to look back over several decades to find writers of this level of "significance." As to contemporaries: Amis, Osborne, Gunter Grass, Philip Roth, Robbe-Grillet . . . no one among these shows any sign of developing the stature of a Shaw or Joyce. We simply take it for granted that nothing much has happened for decades. In 1902, things *had* been happening for decades, and they showed no sign of slackening; the age of Dickens and Carlyle gave way to the age of Stevenson, Hardy, Meredith, and Kipling. The English were discovering Tolstoy and Dostoevsky, Strindberg, Ibsen, Zola, Nietzsche, and Maeterlinck. Things seemed to be happening everywhere; it was a great melting pot, shooting off sparks of literary talent. It was still a romantic era, as lively as the *Sturm und Drang* period of a hundred years earlier—except that the romanticism now had a distinctly optimistic flavour. By the time this era came to an end—in 1914—Tolkien was twenty-two, and his formative period was over.

I strongly suspect that Chesterton was the major influence during this period. The clues are scattered throughout the essay *On Fairy-Stories* (delivered at St. Andrews in 1938). Speaking, for example, about suspension of disbelief, the "enchanted state" which some people can achieve when watching a cricket match, he says: "I can achieve (more or less) willing suspension of disbelief, when I am held there and supported by some other motive that will keep away boredom: for instance, a wild, heraldic preference for dark blue rather than light"—a sentence that could easily have been written by Chesterton. He speaks about one of the important functions of the fairy story, to produce a state of "recovery," "regaining of a clear view." He then goes on to speak of *"Mooreeffoc"* or Chestertonian fantasy, "the queerness of things that have become trite, when they are seen suddenly from a new angle."

Readers of early Chesterton books will recollect that Disneyland atmosphere. "It was one of those journeys on which a man perpetually feels that now at last he must have come to the end of the universe, and then finds he has only come to the beginning of title—grows up to become a wanderer between the village and the land of Faery. Various adventures are described—with a brevity and arbitrariness uncharacteristic of Tolkien—and at the end of the story, the smith hands back the star, his passport to Faery land, and it is passed on to another child through the Great Cake. The apprentice turns out to be the King of the Faery in disguise. All this is fairly clear. The Cooks who make the Great Cake are somehow the intermediaries between the Faery and "the world" (it is Tolkien who makes the distinction); perhaps they are story tellers. The children who swallow the star are the poets—like Yeats or Tolkien—who become wanderers between two worlds. Apart from an earlier fable, *Leaf by Niggle,* this is the most "symbolic" of Tolkien's stories, scarcely a children's story at all. The content is hardly profound; in some ways, it could be called naive; it might have been a story by Walter de la Mare, with its simple message of turning away from the everyday world. In fact, only one step away from *Peter Pan.* Yet naive or not, the problem Tolkien is writing about is fundamental, and its importance and relevance have not diminished since the time of Yeats and Barrie. This is a point that Edmund Wilson completely failed to grasp in his essay.

There are a few more "influences" to be noted. The period of Chesterton's early books was also the period of Belloc's *Path to Rome* (1902), the kind of travel book that can be enjoyed even by people who hate travel books. Belloc describes how he finished his military service at Toul, in Alsace, and decided to walk across Switzerland to Rome. There are sketches—by Belloc himself—of great misty views, and the front cover of the first edition (which I bought years ago for two shillings) has a colored inset of a blue sky with white clouds and a road that goes through a forest on a mountainside. It is "escape" literature in the best sense, and Belloc never again captured that same invigorating sense of freedom and great open vistas, although he tried hard in *Four Men* and *The Cruise of the Nona.* I have no idea whether Tolkien ever read *The Path to Rome,* but it seems to me that this book above all others could have triggered his lifelong obsession with journeys and heroes who set out to walk towards the mountains.

So, I think, could the work of another writer whose work is never mentioned by respectable critics: Jeffrey Farnol. His first book, *The Broad Highway,* came out in 1910, and brought him overnight fame, running into endless impressions. Farnol used the same plot again and again, always with a certain success, for it possesses a potent charm—the young man setting out on the open road with a few shillings in his pocket, in search of romance, adventure, and fortune. Anyone who read Farnol in his teens will never forget him. He must have tempted many children to run away from home. Tolkien was eighteen when *The Broad Highway* appeared; I find it inconceivable that he did not read the book and find it absorbing.

Another influence—of Anglo-Saxon and medieval poetry—is altogether more obvious, and, in my view, less important. Tolkien began as a philologist. Edmund Wilson quotes a statement prepared

Tufnell Park, London died away in draggled taverns and dreary scrubs, and then was unaccountably born again in blazing high streets and blatant hotels. . . ." What Chesterton is describing here (in *The Blue Cross*) might have come out of a novel by Graham Greene; but the way in which he describes it makes it somehow mysterious and exhilarating. Dickens occasionally commanded that magic and J.B. Priestley catches it in a few of his novels. Tolkien set out to take it out of "this world," to create it in isolation, or rather, in its own setting, in "fairy land."

This immediately suggests another name—W.B. Yeats. Not only because Yeats wrote about fairies, but because he attached a particular symbolic meaning to them. There is a sharp dichotomy in Yeats between "this world" and a world of deeper *meaning* that poets glimpse in moments of intensity. The dichotomy between "this world" and that more meaningful reality is a false one; what is at issue is an *attitude,* like the difference between Greene and Chesterton. In certain exhilarated moods, the poet sees the world as endlessly exciting and interesting; in such states of insight, it seems clear to him that all one needs is intelligence and imagination, and the vision can be renewed every day. The really baffling thing is why this vision is so difficult to sustain. The straightforward view is that most human beings are tied down to dreary everyday affairs, like Dickens in his blacking factory or Wells in his drapery emporium, and that all the embryonic Dickenses and Wellses need is freedom. We soon discover that the problem is more complicated than that; even intelligent and imaginative men are often bored. For some reason, this sense of the world as an endlessly meaningful place slips away from us when we need it most. Boredom is one of the great mysteries of psychology. It seems to be a matter of *focussing,* like focussing a very powerful microscope or telescope; and we are just not very good at focussing. "Focussing" occurs in moods of serenity or of creative excitement. Its greatest enemy is the ordinary, noisy distractions of everyday reality. So in his early poetry, Yeats continually attacks this reality—"The wrong of unshapely things is a wrong too great to be told" (echoing the forger Wainewright, who murdered his sister-in-law because he said he couldn't stand her thick ankles)—and creates a world of misty trees and autumn leaves and men who wander off into the land of the Faery. And seventy or so years after Yeats wrote "The Song of Wandering Aengus," Tolkien produced *Smith of Wootton Major,* a fable that might have been published in the Yellow Book with Aubrey Beardsley drawings. Wootton Major is one of those rustic villages in an unnamed country that might be next door to Hobbit-land, and the Great Cook of the village produces a magnificent cake every twenty-four years. But when the story opens, the present cook has been wandering off for mysterious absences (from which he returns merrier than usual), and he finally goes away permanently, leaving behind a strange apprentice whom he has brought back from his wanderings. Next time the Great Cake is baked, the apprentice slips into it a silver star—a fairy gift—and one of the children swallows it. This child—the [black]smith of the

An Ent

for his publishers in which Tolkien refers to *The Lord of the Rings* as a philological game. "The 'stories' were made rather to provide a world for the languages than the reverse." This, it seems to me, is a red herring, like James's description of *The Turn of the Screw* as "a fairy tale, pure and simple." Tolkien may well have derived enormous pleasure from giving the book another dimension of realism with the invention of Elvish and other "languages," but this modest statement of its aims is plainly an attempt to disarm hostile critics—as it partly disarmed Wilson.

The influence of Anglo-Saxon and medieval poetry on Tolkien is quite clear. To begin with, there is his strong tendency to a backward-looking nostalgia, derived in part from Chesterton and Belloc, and their "two acres and a cow" Distributism. Next there is the pleasure in the sensual quality of life in the Middle Ages, as portrayed in its poems—great sides of beef cooking over open fires, magnificent feasts, colorful festivities, and so on. Finally, there is the element of savagery and wildness: the great battles, the burning of Njal, the bleak open moorlands and the lakes that hold monsters like Grendel (perhaps the creepiest monster in literature outside Frankenstein). It is very much an idealized, Chestertonian medievalism, rather like that of T.H. White. From *The Lord of the Rings,* one would gather that Tolkien's interest in the Middle Ages is literary and idealistic; not precise and detailed, like that of G.G. Coulton and Huizinga. And it could be argued that the battle scenes of *The Lord of the Rings* spoil the total effect, that they seem to be part of a completely different book. They certainly interrupt the swift flow of the story. When I first read *The Lord of the Rings* I skipped the whole of the fifth book in order to find out what happens after Frodo is captured by the Orcs, and when I later read it aloud to my children, they again insisted on skipping it. On this occasion, I returned to the fifth book after I had got Frodo and Sam on their road to Mount Doom, but the children seemed to lose interest until we got back to Frodo and Sam.

Finally—in considering "influences"—one should point out the relationship between Tolkien and T.S. Eliot. *The Waste Land* is an attack on the modern world, and Eliot turns to the past for his symbols of a superior order of reality—the Fisher King, the Rhine maidens, the Grail legend, "inexplicable splendour of Ionian white and gold."

In the essay on fairy tales, Tolkien has some strong words defending the fairy story against charges of "escapism." He mentioned that he recently heard "a clerk of Oxenford" declare that he welcomed "the proximity of mass-production robot factories, and the roar of self-obstructive mechanical traffic because it brought his university into 'contact with real life'. . . ." This view obviously makes Tolkien see red. "He may have meant that the way men were living and working in the twentieth century was increasing in barbarity at an alarming rate, and that the loud demonstration of this in the streets of Oxford might serve as a warning that it is not possible to preserve for long an oasis of sanity in a desert of unreason by

Standing Stone on the Barrow Downs

mere fences, without actual offensive action (practical and intellectual). I fear he did not. In any case the expression 'real life' in this context seems to fall short of academic standards. The notion that motor cars are more 'alive' than, say, centaurs or dragons is curious; that they are more 'real' than, say, horses is pathetically absurd.'' One sentence has a positively Chestertonian ring: "Fairy stories may invent monsters that fly the air or dwell in the deep, but at least they do not try to escape from heaven or the sea.'' He argues that talk about "escapism" is a misuse of language: why shouldn't a man in gaol try to escape? What he is arguing here—although he does not put it in so many words—is that there is escape *from* reality and escape *to* reality, and that what interests him is the escape *to* reality. It is Yeats's argument with the "socially conscious" writers of the thirties all over again.

In the same volume as the essay on fairy stories (*Tree and Leaf*) Tolkien includes a short fable, "Leaf by Niggle," written shortly after publication of *The Hobbit* (1937). This is an odd little work, almost Kafka-esque. It begins typically "There was once a little man called Niggle, who had a long journey to make." But this is not another story of man's search for fairy land. Niggle is a painter who is engaged on a picture that sounds like an illustration for *The Lord of the Rings*—mountains, forests, lakes, with an enormous tree in the foreground, a kind of Tree of Life. Niggle is often interrupted by a tiresome neighbor, Parish, a lame man with a sick wife. Parish's only interest is in digging his garden, and he finds Niggle's neglect of his own garden annoying. When he calls on Niggle, he does not even glance at the picture of the tree and fairy landscape. So far, the symbolism is clear enough: Niggle, the visionary artist, but nevertheless a modest little man, working away quietly, minding his own business, trying to capture his vision of fairy land, the "world of meaning," and Parish, the man-in-the-street, interested only in "practical" things and always obstructing the artist.

Parish interrupts Niggle as he is trying to finish the picture, and asks him to go and get a doctor for his sick wife. Niggle goes, gets caught in a storm, and catches a cold that confines him to his bed for weeks, destroying his chance of finishing the picture before he sets out on his journey. While he is in bed, a strange Kafka-esque official calls on him and tells him that his neighbor's house is not satisfactory—the implication being that it is Niggle's duty to take care of his neighbor. Niggle's picture would be just the right size to mend a hole in Parish's roof. When Niggle protests "It's *my* Picture," the Inspector replies "I dare say it is. But houses come first. That is the law." The bewildered artist is ordered to start on his journey, and he sets out quite unprepared. The journey is pure Kafka; he is pushed on to a train, gets out at a station where the porter yells "Niggle," collapses, and is taken to a workhouse infirmary. This turns out to be a kind of prison where he is made to do boring manual tasks (it sounds like a Soviet labor camp) and spends hours locked in his room in the dark. Then some mysterious "judges" talk about him so he can overhear them. Niggle, it seems, is at fault; but the judges finally agree that he is a good sort and deserves a second chance. "He took a great deal of pain with leaves." So Niggle is let out, and sent on another train journey. This time he finds himself in a kind of Happy Land where his tree is an actuality, and behind it is the visionary country of his picture. His old neighbor Parish—who has also been confined in the workhouse for negligence—joins him, and they now work together to build a cottage with a garden. When this is finished—by this time Niggle has become the practical man and Parish something of a dreamer and slacker—Niggle finally goes off towards his goal in the mountains, leaving Parish to live in the cottage with his wife.

Back in Niggle's old house, only a corner of his canvas remains, a single leaf, and this is put into the museum (hence the title of the story). The place that has been created by Niggle and Parish in cooperation becomes known as "Niggle's Parish."

It is an odd little story, most disappointing to children. The "journey" is quite plainly death—in fact, Tolkien makes something say so at the end of the story, where a councilor remarks that Niggle was worthless to society, and ought to have been sent on his journey much earlier, and consigned to the great Rubbish Heap. Like Yeats, Tolkien is continuing his argument with the socially conscious writers of the thirties. But what precisely is he saying? Niggle is an artist and something of a visionary, but all in a rather bumbling, incompetent manner. This incompetence seems to be the root of his trouble. If he were more ruthless, he would tell Parish to go to hell, and finish his picture. But this, Tolkien implies, is the wrong solution. The Niggle-Parish conflict is not really necessary; they *can* collaborate fruitfully, and when they do, it becomes clear that Niggle is Parish's superior.

The final judgment, then, is unexpectedly complex. In the conflict between the artist and society, Tolkien comes down on the artist's side—as is to be expected—but he also blames the artist, implying that if he were less vague and incompetent, he could become something more like a leader of society—without, however, compromising his own basic vision. He does not have to become a servant of the State and paint pictures of tractors. . . . But what precisely he *is* supposed to do is left to the imagination.

This brings us back to the assertion in the essay on fairy stories, that it is not possible to preserve an oasis of sanity in a desert of unreason "without actual offensive action (practical and intellectual)." That is fine; but what offensive action? As far as I can see, Tolkien nowhere suggests an answer to this problem. His own "defensive action" was justifiable enough if we accept Connolly's view that the artist's business is to produce a masterpiece. For all its sentimentality and its flaws, *The Lord of the Rings* is a masterpiece. Whether it has any practical significance for the present discussion of the artist and society is a different matter.

It seems to me that if we reject Edmund Wilson's view that Tolkien's work is an overgrown children's story of no significance, and accept that it is a part of the great European romantic tradition, attacking the same problems as the tales of Hoffmann, Goethe's *Faust*, De L'Isle Adam's *Axel*, Hesse's *Steppenwolf*, Eliot's *The Waste Land*, then we must admit that Tolkien has weakened his own case by sticking too close to fairy tale traditions. I believe that *The Lord of the Rings* is a significant work of twentieth-century literature, as significant as *Remembrance of Things Past* or *The Waste Land*. Its extraordinarily wide appeal—on American campuses, for example—is not due to purely "escapist" elements. It strikes a chord, as *The Waste Land* did in the twenties, because its symbols constitute a kind of *exploration* of the real world. We still live under a threat of a great oppressive evil. But all imaginative people feel that there are solutions that no politician is far-sighted enough to grasp. Our hope for the future lies in the capacity of the human imagination to reach beyond the present, in our capacity to glimpse vistas of meaning that stretch out endlessly around us. Tolkien's work performs the important function of stimulating this wild, Chestertonian hope for the future. For all I know, Tolkien may have thought of himself as a pessimist, in the strictly historical sense; i.e. he may have seen no practical hope for our civilization. But in the fairy tale essay, Tolkien states that one of the most important functions of the fairy tale is to aid "recovery"; that is to say, the work of fantastic imagination may be regarded as a kind of hospital, a place where exhausted people can regain strength and hope.

But, I repeat, Tolkien has, to some extent, undermined his own case: primarily, by sticking to the tradition of "the little man."

Presumably there is a psychological reason for this: Tolkien feels that the quiet, modest chap, who is capable of heroic exertion under stress, is a more satisfactory hero than Siegfried or Lancelot. There may be some truth in this: but in the way it is worked out in *The Hobbit* and *The Lord of the Rings,* it furnishes ammunition for critics who acuse him of sentimentality. In fact, I suspect that Tolkien's choice of the "little" hero may have been largely a matter of pure chance. Tolkien's work "snowballed"; it grew by accident. One can see this process clearly in the various books from *The Hobbit* to *Smith of Wootton Major* (1967). *The Hobbit,* like *Alice in Wonderland,* began as a story for children—literally a story told to his own children. Stylistically, it has a casual, careless air. This style is very different from the slightly pretentious style of *Smith of Wootton Major,* which is a little too obviously biblical and poetical.

The story is also distinctly tailored for children. The comforts of the hobbit-hole are listed, and Tolkien enjoys talking about tea and toast and cakes in front of a roaring fire; it is very much a Walt Disney kind of world. When the dwarfs (or dwarves, as Tolkien prefers to call them, for some philological reason) start arriving one by one, until the house is overflowing with them, you can imagine the children squealing with laughter, and saying "How many more?"

The basic Tolkien formula emerges very quickly. There is a certain realism in the descriptions of difficult journeys, reminiscent of *The Thirty Nine Steps* or *Kidnapped.* He likes describing travels through imaginary landscapes, and he produces the same blend of poetry and adventure and discomfort that one finds in Belloc. He has an excellent imagination for sudden adventures, like the scene with the trolls in the second chapter of *The Hobbit,* where the whole party nearly ends up being eaten by these hairy monsters. The grown up reader finds it exciting because the trolls are sufficiently like gangsters or Nazi thugs to produce the sense that we are talking about something real. Already, Tolkien is showing the ability to write on two levels—for children and adults—that makes *The Lord of the Rings* so successful. One might say that Tolkien had made the important discovery that there is really no need to assume that children and adults have different tastes; what will excite one will excite the other. Also worth noting is that the scene with the trolls is pulled back from the edge of being too "scarey" for children with the comic climax out of "The Brave Little Tailor"—the trolls being induced to fight among themselves by imagining that one of their number is playing tricks on the others.

Towards the end, the book begins to lose impetus as a "fairy story"; the events slow down; the wait on the Lonely Mountain is altogether more "real" than the earlier scenes. In the conventional fairy story, Bilbo Baggins would kill the dragon by a clever stratagem; in *The Hobbit,* the dragon is killed almost arbitrarily "off stage" by Bard, one of the lake men. The quarrel that then follows—between the dwarves, who have now regained their treasure, and the lake men—is again a realistic touch, indicating that

Tolkien is beginning to enjoy the adventure—and battle—for its own sake. Any good literary psychologist might have prophesied that *The Hobbit* would be followed by a more carefully realistic novel. And from the unflagging invention of *The Hobbit,* he might also have guessed that it would be longer.

According to Tolkien, *The Lord of the Rings* was begun shortly after publication of *The Hobbit* (1938-9). *The Fellowship of the Ring* appeared in 1954, so its genesis was lengthy. This is apparent in the book itself, which gradually changes tone as it goes along. The opening, with the great birthday party, might have been written by Edith Nesbit, or even Enid Blyton; it is still very much in the spirit of a tale told for children. One gets the feeling that Bilbo's sudden disappearance—as he slips on the ring—was not really a calculated part of the story; it is still in the jolly, slapstick spirit of the opening of *The Hobbit.* One can also understand perfectly why it was that Tolkien had no ideas about the development of the plot. His heroes were Setting Off, walking into the unknown, like Belloc or the heroes of Jeffrey Farnol, or Hermann Hesse. The spirit here is very close to Farnol; all the talk about the Brandywine river and the pleasant home comforts of Hobbits are all rather sentimental and "twee." Tolkien seems to have invented a kind of secular paradise, a lazy man's heaven, where people have nothing to do but smoke their pipes in the twilight and gossip about the courting couples and next year's May Fair. This paradisial quality is underlined by the information that Hobbits live a great deal longer than human beings— Bilbo is celebrating his eleventy-first birthday. There can be no doubt that Tolkien himself is emotionally committed to this fairy tale picture of peaceful rural life; it is not intended solely for the children.

I imagine that a critic like Wilson would find the first book enjoyable enough, but might begin to grow restive at the Council of Elrond, where one feels that Tolkien is at last beginning to take himself seriously, interposing his own values and writing imitation Norse-saga. He seems to be facing his critics and asking, "Wasn't their world preferable to ours?" And it is purely a matter of personal feeling. Like Auden, I do not mind sharing the fun, and agreeing for the sake of argument. Another reader may find the style of the speeches unbearably bogus. When Tolkien makes his characters talk a language that might be called Heroicese, some readers feel distinctly "turned off." In fact, I found myself skipping these long speeches when I read the book to my children.

All the same, they do not occupy all that much space. The excitement of the book lies in the journey, and in Tolkien's invention. Like the painter Niggle, Tolkien is definitely a creator of scenery. This is all so strongly realized that one feels he ought to collaborate with an illustrator of genius, or perhaps a whole series of illustrators (as in some editions of Shakespeare that have paintings by practically every major Victorian artist). Wilson objects that none of the characters come alive, and this may be true; but the scenery makes up for it. Tolkien obviously has a very unusual faculty of visualising places: Helm's Deep, Lorien, the White Mountains, the Dead Marshes, the plain of Gorgoroth. Purely as an imaginary travel book, *The Lord of the Rings* is a very remarkable work.

Either you become involved in the fantasy or you don't. If everything in the book "came off" as Tolkien intends it to, it would certainly be one of the masterpieces of all time. And on a first reading, most of it *does* come off, because the suspense keeps the reader moving so fast that he hardly notices when effects fall flat. On second reading, as he lingers over some of the excellent descriptions of forests and rivers, he begins to notice that Tom Bombadil is rather a bore (which one might expect of a man who goes around yelling "Hey dol, merry dol" etc.), that Lothlorien and its elves are a sentimental daydream, that Minas Tirith and its brave fighting men would like an Errol Flynn movie. The core of the book remains Frodo's journey, and this continues to be exciting even after several readings.

But, "objectively" speaking, *can* one explain the extraordinary appeal of *The Lord of the Rings?* Well, on the simplest level one might regard it as a combination of science fiction and the novel of suspense. Now science fiction is notoriously badly written. It is almost impossible to name a science fiction novel written in the past thirty or forty years (that is, since *Amazing Stories* made the genre so popular) that rises above the clichés of cheap pulp fiction. Even some of the genuine classics of fantasy and suspense, like Merritt's *Seven Footprints to Satan* or the novels of Lovecraft, are so badly written that one must simply accept the atrocious style as a sort of convention. For the average literature—if only moderately sophisticated—reader (say an American college student), Tolkien's style and erudition must make a refreshing change. His world has the charm of innocence, reviving memories of childhood, and the magic of escapism in the nonpejorative sense—the open road, danger and hardship. If one assumes that it belongs on the same shelf as Edgar Rice Burroughs, E.R. Eddison, John Taine, Lovecraft, Van Vogt, then it obviously deserves very high marks indeed.

But unlike the writers of science fiction, Tolkien's purpose is not simply to "astonish." As we have seen in the essay on fairy stories, he dislikes the modern world, and like Eliot or Yeats, is allowing this negative feeling to trigger a *creative* response. Although it may sound pretentious to say so, *The Lord of the Rings* is a criticism of the modern world and of the values of technological civilization. It asserts its own values, and tries to persuade the reader that they are preferable to current values. Even the "poetry," which everybody admits to be no better than average, underlines the feeling of seriousness, that even if the landscapes and adventures bear a superficial resemblance to Edgar Rice Burroughs's Martian novels, the purpose goes deeper. This, I think, defines what my early informants about the book were unable to explain: why it can be taken so seriously. In fact, like *The Waste Land,* it is at once an attack on the modern world and a credo, a manifesto. This explains why

Auden can take Tolkien so seriously, although his own poetry seems so deliberately "modern" and anti-escapist.

This comparison raises again the fundamental question. Yeats's fairy poems are very beautiful in their way, but if Yeats had died after he had written them, he would now be merely another minor figure in the 1890s, like Dowson and Johnson. They are valid and important in their way, but Yeats went beyond them. In *Leaf by Niggle,* Tolkien criticises Niggle for ineptitude, for not thinking enough, and it is hard to see any reason why this criticism should not, in the last analysis, be applied to his own work. From an essay on fairy tales to *Smith of Wootton Major* he is stating the same simple proposition: that certain people are dreamers and visionaries, and that although they may seem relatively useless to the community, they embody values that the community cannot afford to forget. This is true enough; but the values embodied in *The Lord of the Rings* are on the same level as those in Yeats's fairy poems. If one is to treat *The Lord of the Rings* as a statement of values, on the same level as the poetry of Eliot or Yeats, or Toynbee's *Study of History,* or the

Warg

novels of Mann or Hesse, then one must agree that it fails because it is soft in the center, a romantic anachronism; it should have been published in the 1850s, not the 1950s. Judged by the standards of George MacDonald's *Phantastes,* or *Alice in Wonderland,* or *The Wind in the Willows,* it is a splendid piece of work that will maintain a permanent place. Judged by the standards of a real work of genius and originality, like David Lindsay's *Voyage to Arcturus,* it lacks that final cutting edge of moral perception and seriousness. It is a fine book, but it does not belong in the first rank.

Tolkien, I suspect, would not mind this judgment in the least. He obviously enjoyed writing it; millions have enjoyed reading it; that, he would say, is enough. You can't expect him to be a Tolstoy or Dostoevsky as well. His position seems to be that the business of the artist—of *his* type of artist—is to create a kind of tree, as green and alive as possible. The tree will serve its purpose in a world that becomes increasingly urbanized.

Within his own terms, he is obviously right. Whether you accept these terms depends upon whether, like Edmund Wilson you feel the artist has a "duty" to the community, to history, to literature, or whatever. My own view of art tends to be less rigorous; I am inclined to feel that there is no point in looking a gift horse in the mouth. No doubt *The Lord of the Rings* is less significant than it looks at first sight. Perhaps it could have been made more significant if Tolkien had seriously thought out the ideas he expressed in *Leaf by Niggle.* But perhaps if he had brooded too much on the artist's relation to society, the book wouldn't have got written at all; and then everybody would be worse off.

Dinner in the Dead Marshes

The Silmarillion *is the heart of J.R.R. Tolkien's invented mythology. With its publication, and that of Humphrey Carpenter's authorized biography, major areas of Tolkien's life and work have now been presented to the public. In the essays that follow, William Cater traces the history of* The Silmarillion, *while Kenneth Atchity sheds light on some of the work to come.*

The Filial Duty of Christopher Tolkien

by William Cater

We called it his last work, but *The Silmarillion* was his first work as well; it must have filled and coloured every part of his life for 60 years. I first heard John Ronald Reuel Tolkien talk about it 11 years ago, and the story in his mind and his notebooks was 50 years old then. I remember sitting in his study, which was the converted garage of his house in Sandfield Road, Oxford, and listening to Tolkien, creator and first inhabitant of that beneficently enchanting world of Middle Earth. He was wandering up and down, endlessly striking matches to light the pipe he was never without, and talking through it, and round it, and sometimes *to* it, and to me, and frequently over my head, about that long-awaited next book.

"It's all rather tragic . . . I'm trying to work in some humour but of course that's hard in mythology," he was explaining. "There's a quarrel in heaven, as it were . . . a battle between the elves and the Dark Lord . . . everything breaking down and failing. And I've got to go into the theology of the place, how they thought it was created. I'm a pedant; everything has to be worked out."

You must imagine this punctuated and interrupted by diggings into a tobacco pouch, by puffings and pauses, the scraping of matches and rattlings of a matchbox, and the old man's sudden grin that would charm birds off trees.

He died with that book still unfinished, and Christopher, his son and literary executor, finally put it together. I talked to Christopher about it, not in a converted garage but in the boardroom of the publishers, Allen & Unwin, who reckon that Tolkien has sold around five million copies in English alone. They are making a first hardback print for *The Silmarillion* of half a million copies, which is five times the normal order for a new book by a best-selling author.

It was *The Silmarillion* which made it difficult to pay a social call on J.R.R. Tolkien during the last years of his life—though he was a most sociable man and a courteous and fascinating host and by no means reluctant to be distracted from more earnest matters for the pleasures of conversation. But to eat with Tolkien (who had a healthy, Hobbit-like appetite), to drink with him (though once a beer man, in his last years he favoured a particular brand of green-ginger wine, very warming and, with or without whisky, astonishingly alcoholic), to listen to him (on parallels between Latin and his own invented Elvish language, on the slender chances which prevented Gothic becoming the language of all Europe, on anecdotes of dons long dust)—all this was delightful but accompanied, like so many pleasures, by a guilty conscience.

For one knew that he was writing—or at least he was *supposed* to be writing—*The Silmarillion;* one might as well consider dropping in on Dickens while he was struggling to complete *The Mystery of Edwin Drood,* or contemplate ringing up Count Tolstoy to say: "I know you're working on a sequel to *War and Peace,* Leo, but how about a bite and a drink on Thursday?"

Not that *The Silmarillion* was a sequel; more interestingly it was a precursor. It was the heart of Tolkien's invented mythology, the scarcely visible roots from which grew the great tree of *The Lord of the Rings*, the source of his invented languages, the origin of his invented peoples, elves, hobbits, ents, dwarves, orcs. As Tolkien would patiently explain, there could not be a successor to *The Lord of the Rings,* for that book ends with evil, embodied as the Dark Lord, destroyed; or rather, dispersed . . . "Black against the pall of cloud, there rose up a huge shape of shadow, impenetrable, lightning-crowned, filling all the sky. Enormous it reared above the world, and stretched out toward them a vast threatening hand, terrible but impotent: for even as it leaned over them, a great wind took it, and it was all blown away, and passed. . . ."

When evil ceases to be concentrated but becomes spread thin through the world, we are no longer in the black and white of mythology, no longer in the world Tolkien created, but in our own real world where all the shades are grey. So the next book could not be a sequel, though sometimes—only a poet and philologist would dare—he called it a 'prequel'.

Christopher, now in his early fifties, remembers "among my earliest literary recollections are my father telling me stories from *The Silmarillion;* all the major stories were in being before *The Lord of the Rings* was written. The whole idea goes back to the 1920s, and the earliest tales in it were written during the First World War, 'in army huts, crowded, filled with the noise of gramophones', he once told me, and some lines were scribbled on the back of a paper setting out the chain of responsibility in a battalion.

"The idea grew with him and he was continually developing its meaning, but he tended to work on a story by starting again at the beginning, so one might find a complete version of a very early date, and then another version in which most of that was rewritten, and then another version in which part of *that* was rewritten, and then another . . . layer upon layer. One of the tasks necessary to produce the book out of all this was to find a median level in style, for some parts were in the original version and others so worked over that the styles did not match.

"As his life went on, the mythology and poetry in my father's work sank down behind the philosophy and theology in it . . . his elves were becoming steadily less elvish, for example. He was still writing substantial notes the year before he died, but much of his thought in his last 10 years was devoted to explaining things in his own work as though it were something he had discovered rather than something he had created and could alter. He once said that in writing he had a sense of recording what was already there, somewhere, not inventing it, and where there were discrepancies between things he had written, he sought to study more deeply what he had already written in order to reconcile them."

Christopher recalls, as an example, the Tolkien character who apparently lived twice; killed in *The Silmarillion* he later reappears alive and well in *The Lord of the Rings*. This two-lives character is one of Tolkien's elves who, though immortal in the sense of being

The Horn of Helm's Deep

ageless, are capable of being killed. "A year before his own death my father was writing to explain this, going into the implications of elvish immortality; it turned into a theological discussion.

"This sort of thing made the book too complicated to be publishable by my father. Part of my task was to let the stories stand for themselves and not allow too much philosophy or detail overcome them."

I asked whether he didn't feel rather overwhelmed by the task of producing the book that, in a lifetime, his father could not. Christopher paused to relight his pipe. Though he uses less tobacco and certainly fewer matches—his father's pipesmoking was a pyrotechnic display in aid of Bryant and May—it is a mannerism similar to that of his father; in certain ways the likeness between the two is very strong. Then he said No, he didn't feel overwhelmed.

As the one of Tolkien's four children who went into the same profession, as an academic at the same university and in the same subject (Anglo-Saxon) he was close to his father's thinking. "I am the person most likely to know what he was about. And the knowledge that he wanted me to be his literary executor gave me the confidence to do it. I could not help him in his lifetime as much as I wished, for just to sort out his papers, which were in an enormous mess, would have meant asking him to step aside from them for a year or two. Since his death I've seen far more of his total literary and moral purpose than before. I've had his whole opus spread out

in front of me, letters, papers, essays—more than he ever had, because of the confusion his papers were in.''

Preparing the book was a scissors-and-paste task, Christopher says, though ''because there were often so many versions of the same story from which to select, there's a great deal of my own personal literary judgment in the book. But only very small amounts of linking material had to be written, and in those nobody is made to say or do anything my father didn't intend them to.''

Christopher gave up his Oxford post to concentrate on the book and now does not wish to return. ''My father's invented languages, though enormously complicated, are of more interest than the rather well-tramped field of Anglo-Saxon. I would like to go on to prepare the remaining material, other versions of stories in prose and poetry. But there isn't a fourth work by J.R.R. Tolkien.''

Towards the end of his life Tolkien knew he was not going to finish *The Silmarillion;* but he was content that Christopher would do so. It was a situation that he had perhaps predicted 25 years earlier when, in *The Lord of the Rings*, the elderly hobbit, Bilbo, is dozing by the fire and leaves a young kinsman the task of completing his history of Middle-earth. There were certainly times in those last years when, shut in his study and ostensibly working on the enormous manuscript, Tolkien instead relaxed by painting the beautiful tiles, textiles or coats of arms of his imaginary world.

There was, I think, an insoluble problem in this first and last work which might have daunted him. Much of the power of *The Lord of the Rings* lies in its balance between wild fantasy and plain detail. The author once growled to me that he couldn't stand ''those old romances where a knight in full armour sets off on a journey without even a cake in his hand.'' Tolkien's characters always packed their provisions with care. There is an immense reality and solidity about his work; his landscapes are three-dimensional. When his characters toil on under weeping skies, you can feel the rain down your own neck. If they come to a hill, it doesn't feel like a hill invented that moment to suit the story, but one which has stood there for all time waiting for the story to reach it.

''He once used the image of a mural painter who paints in places he knows can never be seen—behind the pillars. The amount of working behind any published text of his is incredible,'' said Christopher. ''He would get into problems over where the moon would be at a particular time in the story and what time moonrise would be. The need for this detail doesn't really arise in the new book because the stories there are represented as legends from a very remote antiquity.''

So in the *The Silmarillion* the intense reality, which at once heightens fantasy and makes it more believable, is missing. And there cannot, as Tolkien said, be much lightening of the tone: these legends are about high matters, the strife of the gods, and written in a high style which at best is a medium magnificently fit for the message but at worst becomes wearying; one aches for someone to cook a meal or crack a joke.

All flaws admitted, it is enormously bold: how many authors, since Milton moved in on that particular literary property, have dared make a new creation legend, proud fallen archangel and all? To invent a new Pantheon of gods? A world created from the *music* of the gods? A king who, mad with the fear of death, makes war on heaven and is swept away by a tidal wave while his country sinks, like Atlantis, beneath the waves? This is creation on the grand scale.

After that attempt to take heaven by storm, the home of the gods was removed from earth, says *The Silmarillion,* and from then on if men sailed westward they came no nearer to the blessed land but merely "set a girdle about the earth and returned weary at last to the place of their beginning." Only the few heroes of the struggle against personified evil were allowed to sail their grey ship west "until the seas of the Bent World fell away beneath and borne upon the high airs above the mists of the world it passed into the ancient West and an end was come for the Eldar of story and song."

It will be a long time before that, the first and last story of J.R.R. Tolkien, will be forgotten.

Two Views of
J. R. R. Tolkien

by Kenneth John Atchity

With the posthumous publication of Tolkien's *The Silmarillion,* critical exegesis of one of the most inspired writers in the history of English letters can now begin. The methods of structural analysis, applied by anthropologists, mythographers, linguists, and literary critics, can, and no doubt will, tell us much about the precise configurations of the mind that created Middle-earth. But the measure of the scope and profundity of that mind can be taken now, albeit speculatively and intuitively. Whether or not he proves to be a gigantic influence on literature to come, J.R.R. Tolkien was a literary giant, an epos unto himself. Ironically, he considered himself the very opposite: 'I am in fact a hobbit,' he once wrote, 'in all but size,' ending the brief self-portrait reported in Carpenter's excellent biography: 'I do not travel much.'

Tolkien's worldwide audience, who revere him for their travels through the length and breadth of Middle-earth in *The Hobbit* and *The Lord of the Rings* and even further back through space and time in *The Silmarillion,* may marvel at his xenophobia. But the irony of this description takes on new light when compared with another statement Tolkien made to an interviewer: 'The Hobbits are just rustic English people, made small in size because it reflects the generally small reach of their imagination.' In time and space the reach of Tolkien's imagination far exceeds that of any other in

Tim Kirk's drawings have been popular with Tolkien fans since they first appeared in the early fanzines. His work has reached a wider audience during the past few years, and has earned him a reputation as one of the most talented artists to interpret Tolkien's Middle-earth. These paintings are part of a series of twenty-six which was done for his master's degree in illustration. They first appeared in Ballantine's Tolkien Calendar *for 1975.*

Frodo Meditates

The Riddle Game

Gandalf and Bilbo

Maggot's Farm

Two Orcs

The Road to Minas Tirith

The Cracks of Doom

The Last Shore

western literature, with the possible exception of the authors of the Bible. Other epic masters are certainly more profound in philosophical and psychological sensitivity and penetration. But none has sought to see so far—much farther, in fact, than the recorded vision attests. For the most striking characteristic of the history of the First Age presented in *The Silmarillion* is its allusive incompleteness, intriguing and frustrating the reader with a poignancy heightened immeasurably by the knowledge that the creator of this mythological history will say no more. One suspects that Tolkien never finished his masterpiece because its state of incompletion signalled his own aliveness.

The life-force of its creator is infused in *The Silmarillion*, strikingly apparent in every allusive reference that finds its full explanation only in the silent mind: ' . . . his people lamented him ever after and took no king again.' A story lurks here, begging to be told, exactly as it does in the one-line references that permeate the ancient Greek epic cycle or the lore of the Edda. Those who expected from *The Silmarillion* the fulfillment of the history behind *The Lord of the Rings* don't understand the character of the epic mind: the world it creates always exceeds its own expression of that world.

Comparison to the Bible, on literary grounds, is not exaggerated since the aesthetic that guides both is the same stark combination of mythology and morality that lends the credibility of truth. Carpenter suggests that Tolkien would not have accepted his friend C.S. Lewis's statement that 'myths are lies, even though lies breathed through silver.' Tolkien would follow Aristotle in considering art to be, instead of lies, *mimesis,* authentic imitation (or Recreation) of reality, and would agree with Aristotle's conclusion that, for this reason, 'poetry is more philosophical than history because history shows us only what *was* or *is,* while poetry shows us what *might be* or *should be.'* Carpenter explains: 'And just as speech is invention about objects and ideas, so myth is invention about truth. In expounding this belief in the inherent *truth* of mythology, Tolkien had laid bare the centre of his philosophy as a writer, the creed that is at the heart of *The Silmarillion.*' The resemblance to Biblical literature is apparent on every page, as a random opening demonstrates: 'Then Lúthien stood upon the bridge, and declared her power: and the spell was loosed that bound stone to stone, and the gates were thrown down, and the walls opened, and the pits laid bare . . .' Erich Auerbach (in his essay 'Odysseus' Scar') has described this kind of epic narrative: lean, austere, direct, gathering its stylistic force from name and action, and almost no description. The impression created in the reader is very like religious awe. It is the binding spell woven by what Tolkien calls a successful 'sub-creator,' who lures us into his sub-creation with the sheer power of his language, his mage-like command over the secret rituals of names. Carpenter is precisely correct in seeing Tolkien's childhood linguistic infatuation as the first 'cause' of Middle-earth.

The second force behind Tolkien's achievement was 'his desire to express his most profound feelings in poetry, a desire that owed its origin to the inspiration' of his literary clubmates during WW I, and that owed its realization to the continuation of their influence through The Inklings, the circle formed by Tolkien and Lewis at Oxford which met weekly to read and comment on one another's works in progress. Only with the appearance of *The Silmarillion* does it become clear how much C.S. Lewis, in his Perelandra trilogy and in the chronicles of Narnia, owes to his friend who always suspected and sometimes envied Lewis' rush to publication. But 'The Book of Lost Tales,' as Tolkien called it when he began the first notebook as early as 1917, precedes Lewis, and indeed directly and clearly inspired him. Lewis continuously urged Tolkien to finish and publish it.

But Tolkien would not bend to Lewis' will, or even to his own, because he was engaged in a process Levi-Strauss would have helped him understand and thereby accept: a myth is never finished, until or unless it is dead. The third and overarching force in Tolkien's literary career was nothing less than a 'desire to create a mythology for England.' Perhaps it was his scholarly dissatisfaction with the Arthurian legend for not continuing to provide metaphors applicable to the times; perhaps it was his own Catholic sense of the disproportionate suffering of human life in a universe of recurrent evil. At any rate, he saw a need in English culture, and saw his mission to fill that need: 'Do not laugh!' he would write long after beginning *The Silmarillion*, 'But once upon a time . . . I had a mind to make a body of more or less connected legend, ranging from the large and cosmogonic to the level of romantic fairy-story—the larger founded on the lesser in contact with the earth, the lesser drawing splendour from the vast backcloths—which I could dedicate simply: to England; to my country. It should possess the tone and quality that I desired . . . be redolent of our "air" . . . , and while possessing (if I could achieve it) the fair elusive beauty that some call Celtic . . . , it should be "high," purged of the gross, and fit for the more adult mind of a land long steeped in poetry. I would draw some of the great tales in fullness, and leave many only placed in the scheme, and sketched. The cycles should be linked to a majestic whole, and yet leave scope for other minds and hands, wielding paint and music and drama. Absurd.'

Of course it was an absurd plan for an ordinary man; but Tolkien, like Walt Whitman, had 'multitudes' within him. The narrative voice in *The Silmarillion* is at first elusive. 'And even so it came to pass; but it is not said that Húrin asked ever of Morgoth either mercy or death.'; 'But Manwe moved not; and of the counsels of his heart what tale shall tell? The wise have said . . .'; 'And even the name of that land perished, and men spoke thereafter not of Elenna, nor of Andor the Gift that was taken away, nor of Númenóre on the confines of the world; but the exiles on the shore of the sea, if they turned towards the West in the desire of their hearts spoke of Mar-nu Falmar that was whelmed in the waves, Akallabeth the Downfallen, Atalante in the Eldarin tongue.' We begin to recognize the intonations. It is the voice of the Sub-creator himself, who knows the names and knows the forgetting of the names, because his point of view is everywhere and nowhere.

Tolkien's work was truly evangelical, his mission nonetheless inspired and inspiring for being expressed as poetry rather than as religion. Indeed his poetry is all the more remarkable because it draws almost nothing from his fervent commitment to Roman Catholicism. The explanation begins with his experiences in the trenches during World War I: 'I've always been impressed . . . that we are here, surviving, because of the indomitable courage of quite small people against impossible odds.' From this adolescent impression spring the central characters of the War of the Rings—the Halflings, Periannoth, the Little People, the hobbits. They are a diminished race in a world that is itself, as we learn in *The Silmarillion*, much diminished. In the *Akallabeth,* one of the three tales contained with the central *Valaquenta* (or *Quenta Silmarillion),* we witness a most significant mythographical reversal as a progression closely resembling that from the Tower of Babel to the Deluge reminds us that Tolkien's *mythos* has returned the Golden Age once more to the distant past where it began in ancient Greek and Hebrew mythology. This is Tolkien's strongest anti- or at least un-Christian statement. Yet there is no diminution in the courage of his Halflings. The least particle of Good is sufficient leaven.

In making the hobbits the heroes of the Third Age, Tolkien is performing the didactic function of epic: he is providing us, men of the Fourth Age (and Hesiod's 'Ages of Man' is a suggestive parallel), with imitable models. Our joy in reading him is precisely in this affirmation of the possibility of effective good action in a nonheroic, diminished world. He himself best describes the impact, in his essay 'On Fairy-Stories': 'The consolation of fairy-stories, the joy of the happy ending: or more correctly of the good catastrophe, the sudden joyous "turn" (for there is no true end to any fairy-tale): this joy . . . is not essentially "escapist," nor "fugitive." In its fairy-tale—or otherworld—setting, it is a sudden and miraculous grace: never to be counted on to recur. It does not deny the existence of *dyscatastrophe,* of sorrow and failure: the possibility of these is necessary to the joy of deliverance; it denies (in the face of much evidence, if you will) universal final defeat and in so far is *evangelium,* giving a fleeting glimpse of Joy, Joy beyond the walls of the world, poignant as grief.'

The Silmarillion, in all its parts and in its connecting link to *The Lord of the Rings* (*Of the Rings of Power and the Third Age*), provides the joy of what Tolkien here terms fairy-story in his famous essay and elsewhere myth. It is myth that takes its form from universal myth, as in the *Ainulindale's* description of the creation of the world through an Empedo-clean alternation 'of endless interchanging melodies that passed beyond hearing into the depths and into the heights, and the places of the dwelling of Ilúvatar were filled to overflowing, and the music and the echo of the music went out into the Void, and it was not void.' And, as true myth, Tolkien takes its credibility from its palpable connection with the reality of the earth:

'And it is said by the Eldar that in water there lives yet the echo of the Music of the Ainur more than in any substance else that is in this Earth; and many of the Children of Ilúvatar hearken still unsated to the voices of the sea, and yet know not for what they listen.' There is no question that Tolkien succeeded in his ambition to create a myth.

The question that must remain unanswered in our own time is whether the myth of Middle-earth will play the shaping cultural role Tolkien quietly cast for it. We must wait through the welter of commercial exploitation—most recently Terry Brooks's blatantly derivative *Sword of Shannara*—to see whether Tolkien's myth will no longer be Tolkien's but our own, one that continues to guide the brush and baton and pen of artists for years to come. Will he be to the tradition as a Spenser, a prodigious, magnificent anachronism whose work will survive only in and for itself? Or will Tolkien take his place with Chaucer, Shakespeare, and Milton whose works survive in the very language we use as well as in everything we read in English? An early sign that the latter fate awaits Tolkien is a new epic fantasy, *The Chronicles of Thomas Covenant the Unbeliever* by Stephen R. Donaldson (the trilogy is Donaldson's first appearance on the literary horizon), in which the influence of Tolkien has sparked a vision that seems to have a life, style, and viewpoint of its own (at this writing, I've not yet finished the books). But early signs are never sure signs.

Meanwhile we can be grateful to Christopher Tolkien for serving as the ideal redactor to his father's mythos, allowing it to come first before us unmarred by critical or textual apparatus that, for the moment, would only distract us from the primary joy of appreciation. We look forward to his editions of Tolkien's unpublished narrative, linguistic, historical, and philosophical notes on Middle-earth. By the same token Humphrey Carpenter has served us well with a thorough and sincere biography that allows us to see the man as clearly and simply as the reverence we share with Carpenter permits and dictates. The next steps are more complicated, more objective, more controversial, less exciting.

The Lord of Rohan

Part II. Frodo Lives:
A Look at Tolkien Fandom

Middle-earth is a world with a history and a mythology all its own. And since the late sixties, Tolkien societies, Tolkien "fanzines," and individual Tolkien fans have been adding to its lore. Tolkien admirers have created Middle-earth sculptures and paintings, Middle-earth embroideries, and Middle-earth costumes; they've organized huge Middle-earth conventions and small Middle-earth feasts; they've produced musical revues, journals, newspapers, books of poems and stories, even collections of "folksongs." The following pages provide a sampling of this activity, and a few sources for new Tolkien fans eager to carry on the tradition.

The Evolution
of Tolkien Fandom

by Philip W. Helms

In one sense, Tolkien fandom predates the actual publication of J.R.R. Tolkien's monumental works of fantasy, *There And Back Again,* and *The Downfall of the Lord of the Rings and The Return of the King.* At times Tolkien's own group, a drinking and literary association called the Inklings (pun intended, as a matter of record), was virtually identical to the fan gatherings that have marked the years since. Directly after publication in the mid 1950s, the circles of the initiated expanded somewhat, but continued to be entrenched largely in professional and professorial circles. Middle-earth was a sort of secret refuge where harried and conservative scholars could meet furtively to swill ale and smoke their pipes while feeling avant-garde and a bit mad.

However, all that crumbled, in the U. S. at any rate, with the advent of the ubiquitous paperback edition. While Ballantine and Ace vied for the market and lawsuits raged, a different element in society took up the several banners of Middle-earth and marched away. Tolkien's works became a campus religion, outselling the *Bible* in 1967 and 1968. As scrawls of "Frodo Lives," "Go Go, Gandalf," and "Sméagol died for your sins" appeared on walls, the earlier segment of fandom deserted like plague-infected rats in a southeast Asian port. A few scholars, embittered, turned to the writing of reviews and articles on this amazing phenomenon. Many attempted to make the works seem inane; most ridiculed the fans and attempted to link them with the "hippie movement," if such a thing ever truly existed. A few were actually honest enough to admit their loss of previous interest—and the reason. The works had been a private refuge, with a certain snob appeal. That was lost, that cloistered, boyish, secret-society quality—and it has never been political for professors to join their students in questionable activities. And naturally Tolkien study was questionable—department heads, presidents, boards of regents, prosperous alumni, and parents all found it quite questionable.

The new wave of fans was comprised largely of students and young people, drawn primarily from college campuses. In 1966, the fan above the age of twenty-five was exceptional. The world was an unsettled place in those days. These were the times of the antiwar protests, of Kent State, of riots (racial and otherwise), of assassinations (Martin Luther King and John Kennedy), and of political madness. The American Dream was crumbling; even the college education which had been held out as a blank check in the 1950s no longer carried assurance of a job. American youth sought a refuge—a system which was not morally grey, a system which would work the way it was supposed to. Some chose the amoral greyness of the counterculture; a few transcended into alien worlds of drug- induced experiences of terror and euphoria. Upon this climate burst the rediscovery of a fine and decent place, a world of clearly defined good and evil with complacent, underachieving heroes—Middle-earth.

The Americans took Middle-earth for their own. They learned to read, write, and speak the languages; they drew maps and posters; they formed clubs and printed bulletins, newsletters, and magazines. An amazed and uncomprehending world gaped. The organizations were a natural outgrowth of this sweeping phenomenon. There was a secrecy and mystery in the works, and a kinship between those initiated, which irresistibly led to the founding of clubs and societies.

Tolkien Societies sprang up like mushrooms after a rain. The designation "Tolkien Society" has been, for more than ten years, the most popular form of organizational name, usually with some geographic modifier. Tolkien Societies can be listed throughout the English-speaking world, and their equivalents elsewhere—including a former "Societas Tolkienis" which was dedicated to, among other things, translation of the works into Latin, and thence to Elvish.

Perhaps the first such group in Europe was The Tolkien Society (Great Britain), which generously accepts members from other nations. To our knowledge, this is the oldest of the European-based organizations. The late professor is perpetual honorary president; the members quietly pursue hobbitlike pastimes and publish *Amon Hen* a bimonthly bulletin of high quality without delusions of grandeur, and *Mallorn,* an occasional journal.

The Tolkien Society of America was founded by Dick Plotz and Ed Meskys in the mid '60s, and used a structure of "smials." Notable among several publications was *Tolkien Journal,* which

passed through many metamorphoses, having been joined variously with *Orcrist* and the Mythopoeic Society. Many smaller groups catered to combinations of interests: Neo-Numenor was a combination war-gaming and Tolkien group not unlike the Dungeons and Dragons groups now current. Eldilla combined Tolkien's world with those of C.S. Lewis, while Empire added E.R. Eddison to Tolkien, Lewis, and war gaming.

Publications also shot up and collapsed again at a great rate. Names like *Mathom Sun, Misty Mountain Monthly, I Palantir, Dormat Dwellers, Entmoot, Triplanetary, Green Nurd Variety, Green Dragon, Anduril, Middle Earthworm,* and *Minas Tirith Evening-Star* hark back to the days when *all* fans published. Consequently,

Ship with the emblem of the Lords of Gondor

ditto and hectograph were the standards of the day, and quality varied enormously. *Minas Tirith Evening-Star,* now the oldest continuing Tolkien publication in America, has had a history the reverse of *Tolkien Journal,* having first been associated with Neo-Numenor, then Eldilla, and after a long period of independence, with the American Tolkien Society.

Independent magazines or other publications were not unusual; to the contrary, in those halcyon days, the well-produced, worthwhile organization publication was a great oddity. All too often, the elaborate structure of kings, stewards, thains, councils, Oyeresu, warlords, wizards, Nazgul, and whatnot led to endless political strife, rivalry, and bickering—all of which took up space and tended to destroy organizations large and small. Sauron was probably quite amused.

The fall of 1967 was a momentous time; August saw the first appearance of *Minas Tirith Evening-Star,* while an enterprising young man named Glen GoodKnight founded the Mythopoeic Society a month or two later. The Mythopoeic Society took the then unlikely tack of studying the Inklings as a whole. Growth was apparently rather slow, if steady, until a 1972 merger with the Tolkien Society of America, following upon the tragic advent of blindness for Ed Meskys. The combined organization, known as the Mythopoeic Society, is now probably the largest U. S.-based fantasy group of this type.

Meanwhile, a curious transformation was occurring. The Tolkien fan had ceased to be the wild man on campus. New instructors began to teach classes on Tolkien, remembering him as philologist and classicist as well as sometime cult hero. The thrust of fandom for new studies and "new information" produced three schools: 1) the analysis of the works as literature and/or religion; 2) the linguisitic and cultural studies dealing with Middle-earth as a real world with a real history; and 3) the elaborationists, who strove to continue the professor's works, with varying degrees of success.

Most influential among this new breed of scholars was a lad named Bob Foster, rumored to live somewhere near Columbia University, under a pile of 3 × 5 index cards. His *Guide to Middle-earth* sparked a revolution that built upon the old standard of devotion: "I've read the trilogy eleven times." The age of esoteric trivia had arrived. Foster, of course, was not alone in this approach. The "scholarly" approach remains quite popular, and sustains many of the Mythopoeic publications in large part. As this new view took over, the elaborationists went into hiding, the wargamers disappeared, the grafitti vanished, the puzzles and games evaporated; even costuming was seriously threatened.

As is the fate of many a movement, however, Tolkien fandom fell into the hands of a new generation. Where once college students dominated the field, high school students and groups have now displaced that preeminence. The commercial success of Dungeons and Dragons and other fantasy war games has revived that area of endeavor, leading to reissuance of the *Rules for the Live Ring Game.* The art has undergone a similar change; when Ballantine drove out Ace, Remington's mishmash became a standard rather than Gaughan's more realistic work. The scholarly phase favored Tolkien's own art, but the here-and-now adores the more-than-photographic reality of the Hildebrandts' works. The day of the smaller group is returning as well, it seems. New organizations are springing up about the country, independent of older and established societies, tailored to meet the needs of a specific group of members. Fervor begins to build to a pitch.

The anticipation prior to the release of *The Silmarillion* produced a renewed interest in elaborations of Tolkien's own work. Several thinly disguised works such as *Sword of Shannara* and *Circle of Light* appeared, to be compared in back cover blurbs to Tolkien's work. Trivia became a game again rather than a way of life; the publications were no longer dominated by the articles of persons seeking degrees in Elvish linguistics or Middle-earth architecture. Even fan publications devoted to hard-core science fiction or to the pulps briefly ran articles and spin-off fiction in the Tolkien field—a practice unheard of for many years. Filmmakers eagerly went back to work on film versions of Tolkien's works, and their influence on other fantasy films is being acknowledged readily by producer and director alike.

The appearance of *The Silmarillion* in September 1977 proved to be anticlimatic for some segments of fandom. The work is far different from the hobbits' adventures; it is morose, brooding, and tragic, harking back far more to the Icelandic sagas than any other single source. Reviewers have been somewhat unsympathetic, and fan reactions have varied widely. What remains has been characterized by Humphrey Carpenter as ''a good bedrock sensible enthusiasm'' and ''a small band of devoted and interested people who share an intelligent and sensitive attitude and interest into Tolkien's books.''

The November 1977 television airing of *The Hobbit,* animated by Rankin and Bass, has stirred a renewed controversy over artistic and dramatic adaptation. While the animated special and the illustrated book based on it have managed to offend some fans, they have created a new level of enthusiasm in the elementary school set. It is tempting to theorize that it is not possible to please, or even avoid offending, all elements of Tolkien fandom in any single undertaking.

The current trend, may it endure, is toward a realistic view of Middle-earth—not for study by archeologists, or dissection by sociologists and theologians, but as a very real place filled with living, breathing people—a place to be experienced rather than scrutinized. With the influence of the Hildebrandts, the animated productions of Rankin and Bass, and of Bakshi, a dimension of life and urgency has returned, like the sun bursting through the overcast of Mordor. We are proud to have been a part of the movement through its many phases and years, as we would have been proud to fight in the long defense of Gondor. But we are prouder still to sound one of the horns that will echo on Mindolluin as the light returns.

Confessions
of a Tolkien Fiend

by Baird Searles

I was one of those lucky people who grew up (literally) with the works of J.R.R. Tolkien and, what's more, grew up with them at a time when only a precious few people knew about them. I first discovered *The Hobbit* in 1944 when I was ten; it immediately became the most important book in my life, to be read and reread.

No need to go into the revelations produced by Tolkien's further books; anyone reading the present volume will know about that. Perhaps the major difference is that all this happened before the onset of the Tolkien cult, and no one today would believe the difficulties involved in persuading anybody to pay attention to Tolkien. *Fantasy* was *Winnie the Pooh* or Harvey, Broadway's invisible (and ultrawhimsical) rabbit. The mention of elves would evoke *A Midsummer Night's Dream* at best, ribald sexual unpleasantness at worst. Lord Dunsany was definitely out of fashion. Any of the few later novels of magical worlds, such as Fletcher Pratt's *The Well of the Unicorn,* was totally unknown save to a few connoisseurs.

Those few patient friends whom I did pressure into reading Tolkien (mainly to shut me up) had predictably varied reactions. A few of the few (the more sensitive, I tend to think) took to them; others returned unimpressed to the real world of the Eisenhower '50s. Then, of course, the picture changed. Going into a New York bookstore to buy a copy of *The Hobbit* for yet another ignorant friend, I encountered a salesgirl who asked if I lived in the East Village. "Everyone in the East Village seems to be reading this book," she informed me. At about the same time, I did a theatrical tour of Midwestern universities and suddenly *more* people who had read Tolkien came into my ken. Then the cultural revolution broke, and *everybody* was reading Tolkien. When I saw the first "Frodo Lives" button, I felt that Things Were Not Going To Be Good, and when everybody and his brother started gabbling about Gollum, nattering about the Nazghul, and blithering about Boromir, I knew it. So I retired from the field, kept my mouth shut, and hoped it would all go away—and of course it hasn't.

In the meantime, I began collecting editions of Tolkien. The psychology of this is, I suppose, fairly obvious. If everybody had to be reading *my* books, at least I could have those books in forms that very few others had. Over the years I have amassed a shelf full. I'm sure there are jet set bibliophiles (if that's not a contradiction in terms) who have far larger collections; I've been content to find my books as I travelled, or allow friends to pick them up for me wherever they might be. I've even made a point of *not* finding out how many languages *The Hobbit* and *The Lord of the Rings* have appeared in since that would set a goal I'd rather not be saddled with.

But what I *do* have displays an amazing variety for one author, and for just two works at that.

There is, of course, the first American edition of *The Hobbit*. Its colored plates are, so far as I know, the only drawings by Tolkien himself that actually show a hobbit. Too bad none of the many who have portrayed hobbits since ever bothered to look at them. The second American edition, still the standard one these days, has only black-and-white drawings, showing buildings and landscapes and, just once, trolls.

The first American *The Lord of the Rings* does not have the now-familiar square of runes-against-flame that is on the current dust jackets. Instead, they picture a bosky dell, the trees curving to enclose the title. On a closer look, you'll find all sorts of odd creatures entwined in the trees: a dragon, a dwarf, a serpent, an owl, and even a gangling creature (presumably an elf) asleep against one of the trunks. What could only be an ent peers coyly from behind another tree. Standing in front of the mythozoological tangle is a hobbit—with an umbrella—looking rather like a beetle in a cutaway coat. While dear to me because they recall a time of great pleasure, objectively I must admit that they leave a great deal to be desired.

The early English wrappers are much more to the point. In fierce red and black on grey, they show the ring (set, alas, with stones) over a black circle. Inside this is the red eye of Sauron, surrounded by runes. The first deluxe edition of *The Lord of the Rings* appeared in England, and it *is* quite beautiful. Although it's still divided into three volumes, no dust jackets are used. Simple black volumes are stamped with gold on the spines, the pages are edged in gold, and the whole set is enclosed in a box decorated on all three sides with a misty mythical landscape that is just right. This drawing also appears on the English one-volume paperback edition.

It was about this time that the first American paperback editions of *The Lord of the Rings* appeared. Now I'm not about to get into the technical, legal, or moral questions raised by the Ace publications. I *will* say that had they not been available at a mere seventy-five cents each, the whole thing might not have gotten out of hand. The covers are pure comic book. On *The Fellowship of the Ring* we find Gandalf perched precariously on a crag, surrounded by jaunty Robin Hood fellows waving swords—which doesn't seem wise considering the balancing act they're all doing. *The Two Towers* cover shows us a Black Rider, also waving a sword. He's riding a rather handsome horse, whose only defect appears to be severely malformed wings. *The Return of the King* sports the same personage (a black cloak with two red eyes) about to embrace a large red stone pillar. In front of him are a motley crew who are yet again brandishing weapons; there are three swords, an axe, and a long stick, the last wielded by a gentleman in the classic wizard's dunce cap, a get-up more than matched by one of the sword wavers, who has a duck on his head. How on earth they attracted *any* readers is beyond me.

On the other hand, I wasn't all that enthralled with the covers on the authorized Ballantine edition. Those peculiar spikey mountains, flora, and fauna are highly regarded by some, but to me they resemble landscapes of the American Southwest rendered by a severely disturbed Navajo.

Not that most of the foreign language paperbacks would take any prizes. Some of them are odd, to say the least; but there *are* the inevitable cultural differences, I suppose. The French edition of *Bilbo le Hobbit,* nevertheless, is one of the ugliest things I have ever seen; it makes the Ace covers look transcendently lyrical. The French idea of a hobbit has curly orange hair (worn somewhat à la Norma Shearer), a curly orange sweater, green and black striped trousers (imparting a sort of *pour le sport* air), and curly orange feet. *Le hobbit* is waving an orange dagger (not, for a change, curly) at a rotund creature vaguely resembling a bear, who is waving back a curly dagger (*not* orange) and an object that may be either a tree limb or a leg of lamb. The bear creature has lots of teeth, as does a wolfish sort who is leaping over the hobbit, perhaps at the leg of lamb. The French edition of the trilogy (*Le Seigneur des Anneaux)* blessedly has no illustration on the covers.

The Dutch paperback covers, appropriately enough, are predominantly in Rembrandtesque browns and greys and are highly stylized, to say the least. Part 1, *De Reisgenoten,* shows a group of astonished hobbits—who are mostly ovals with projecting hands, legs, and heads—eying Frodo, whose invisibility is cleverly suggested by an image that looks as if it's been hastily rubbed out. In the rear sits Aragorn, whose eyes can just be seen between his black cloak and his surprising black cowboy hat. (The Dutch translation of "Ranger" may account for this detail. Behind him the cow jumps over the moon in a green circle that maybe a hobbitish round window. Very odd, as are the other two. But the Dutch name of the second book is irresistible—*De Twee Torens.*

All in all, the Italians come off best. *Lo Hobbit* is a handsome oversized paperback. On the upper half of the front cover, the title and author are printed against a blue ground. Below is a nicely reproduced copy of the color drawing of Bilbo and Smaug. *Il Signore degli Anelli*'s three covers are lovely—brilliantly colored and very abstract landscapes, just vaguely reminiscent of the work of Peter Max.

A foreign edition that should be mentioned, even though I don't own a copy, is the Swedish, illustrated by the wonderful Tove Jansson, whose Moomin books have raised whimsey to a high art. I should think the two styles would be highly incompatible, but their combination must be interesting, if nothing else.

Most American Tolkien lovers are probably aware of the handsome deluxe edition of *The Hobbit* and the one-volume *The Lord of the Rings* published by Houghton Mifflin. Less familiar is the incredibly beautiful one-volume boxed edition of the trilogy brought out in England some years ago. Bound in black, with the golden tree

Emblem of Durin

OVERLEAF: The Lonely Mountain. *A drawing by J. R. R. Tolkien, from Baird Searles's collection of Tolkieniana.*

THE LONELY M

and the ring embossed on the cover, it is less than one and a quarter inches thick, printed on the finest India paper.

The trilogy is in a matching slipcase, and for a change is bound in *white* with abstract Celtic maze designs embossed in gold. Each volume bears the imprint of the Folio Society itself. The illustrations are in black and white, and are almost more decorations than illustrations per se. For the most part, they show only landscapes or objects; the closest they come to portraying a person is in one drawing of a Black Rider (and some would argue with *that* definition). The credit on the title page is somewhat odd, "Illustrations by Ingahild Grathmer, drawn by Eric Fraser."

Behind this lies a tale. "Ingahild Grathmer" is the current Queen Margrethe of Denmark. She had done these drawings while a student in England and submitted them to Tolkien. He evidently approved of them, which was very surprising considering the adamant way he had rejected all other attempts to illustrate his works. (One shudders at what he might have thought of some of the atrocities perpetrated since his death.) The secret of his approval seems to lie in the fact that Her Royal Highness had *not,* with a very few exceptions, attempted to portray the characters, following, as it were, in the footsteps of Tolkien himself.

Why "drawn by Eric Fraser?" The illustrations, as submitted by the Queen, had not been meant for publication and were done in the wrong forms and size. Since she was now subject to the fatiguing schedule and duties that seem to beset royalty, she had no time to redo them, and so Mr. Fraser carefully did the job. Incidentally, Queen Margrethe had agreed to their use only under a pseudonym and on the condition that there would be no publicity attendant on their publication. These conditions were faithfully met by the Folio Society, but in one of those incidents that sometimes make the literary world reminiscent of international espionage, the story was discovered and broken by the Danish press—a sign that the Danes are as nosey about their rulers as are the English.

As you've noticed, a discussion of Tolkien editions inevitably raises the question of illustrating Tolkien. At first thought, Tolkien's works would seem to cry for illustration, but the picturing of fantasy in general and Tolkien in particular is very tricky indeed. One of the subtler talents of the fantasist, and certainly one of the stronger elements in Tolkien's genius, is to make the reader believe the unbelievable. Tolkien made Middle-earth and its inhabitants so very real to us by his words that any attempt to show them concretely is almost foredoomed, save for the evocative style of Tolkien's own drawings.

The latest additions to the collection are almost but not quite so impressive. (No, I do *not* mean that cinemascope-sized book of *The Hobbit* with pictures from the TV movie.) They are the four volumes sold here (by subscription only) by the Folio Society. *The Hobbit* is a lovely brown volume in a slipcase with indented sides that make the book easier to get out. It bears the imprint of Tolkien's English publisher. The illustrations are the familiar drawings from the standard American *Hobbit,* but they're reproduced in color and are beautiful.

A collection of Tolkieniana must, of course, include calendars, which have varied from acceptable to ghastly. I must admit a particular aversion to those done by the Brothers Hildebrandt, which look to me like *tableaux vivants* waxworks which justify reviving that pithy old putdown of the art world, "calendar art."

As for the TV movie of *The Hobbit,* I've yet to talk to a Tolkien lover who could stomach more than a few details of it (the voices of Gollum and Smaug seem to get grudging acceptance). For myself, I found the sound track the most unspeakable part (even more so than the rape of the Arkenstone from the story), what with a warbled "Song of the Hobbit" and a chorus of orcs sounding like Nelson Eddy's men from *Naughty Marietta.* I fled the channel at the appearance of the Wood Elves, who bore an uncanny resemblance to the Dead End Kids of the movies of yore.

It is a slight jump from various editions of Tolkien to various books by other authors that might satisfy the Tolkien reader, but I'd like to make it because I think such a listing might be a public service. As proprietor of The Science Fiction Shop in New York (which means that we carry a large stock of fantasy, since many aficionados read across the genres), I've noticed that many people who love Tolkien don't know where to go from there. While I'd be the first to proclaim that Tolkien is absolutely unmatchable, there are other books (mostly obscure) that have some of the same qualities.

While the following suggested works vary widely in style and approach, please be assured that they all are serious and coherent fantasies; some are supposedly for children, mainly because they have children as protagonists, but still evoke the epic and the magical, and the great battle between good and evil. They are *not* dear little tales of elves at the garden bottom, or dreary allegories intended to painlessly teach mathematics, table manners, or good citizenship. Most are perenially in print, and available at any good bookshop.

Poul Anderson is know primarily for his science fiction, but he has written several wonderful fantasies based on his own Scandinavian heritage. The finest is *The Broken Sword,* set in the tenth century, the very realistic tale of a changeling, a human child captured by elves and raised in the elf mounds. Anderson's elves are amoral and mostly indifferent to man; the major action centers about the great war between the elves of Britain and an invasion of trolls from Scandinavia. Other mythologies are cleverly worked in, including an intriguing chapter about the *tuatha* of Ireland.

Joy Chant tantalized readers for ten years with only one book, *Red Moon And Black Mountain,* set in a magic world like Middle-earth. There, too, a great war is fought, led by Princess In'serinna, an enchantress of the Star Magic who battles Fendarl, the Black Enchanter. Female readers will be particularly happy with In'serinna. Just recently, a companion volume *The Grey Mane Of Morning,* has appeared.

Susan Cooper's *Dark Is Rising* series consists of five books: *Over Sea, Under Stone; The Dark Is Rising; Greenwitch; The Grey King;* and *Silver on the Tree.* In these tales, contemporary English children fend off the magic intrigues of the Dark against the Light, and much depends on several enchanted artifacts—a harp, a sword, and a grail. Help comes from the immortal Merlin, and there are other subtle links to the Arthurian legends.

Lord Dunsany was as cynical and sophisticated as Tolkien was not; nevertheless, he was among the first to work seriously at the creation of worlds of magic and myth. His jewelled, art nouveau prose works best in his many short stories, but in at least one novel, *The King of Elfland's Daughter,* the beauty transcends the irony.

Alan Garner's *The Weirdstone of Brisingamen* and its sequel, *The Moon of Gomrath,* also involves children in an epic conflict between good and evil, but here the battle is waged over a few square miles of countryside. The creatures of fantasy are mostly invisible to adult eyes, and ordinary objects such as scarecrows suddenly and frighteningly manifest malevolent intelligence. Here we meet the lios-alfar, the last of the elves of Britain, dying from the pollution of man; the wonderful dwarves Fenodyree and Durathror; the maggot breed of Ymir, the svarts, as unpleasant as any orcs; and the terrifying female trolls, the mara.

Ursula K. Le Guin is another writer best known for her superlative science fiction, but her Earthsea trilogy *(A Wizard of Earthsea, The Tombs of Atuan,* and *The Farthest Shore)* is set in a magical world of dragons and wizards and awful powers that can be set loose but not so easily controlled. The trilogy concerns the growing into maturity of one wizard, and is notable for its spare and understated style.

C.S. Lewis's *Narnia* series probably needs little introduction. These seven books about the magical country of Narnia are classics, and while the first is cute rather than convincing and the theological content sometimes becomes a bit too thick, there are many moments of magic and grandeur.

As of this writing, Patricia McKillip has only completed two books of a projected trilogy. *The Riddle Master of Hed* and *Heir of Sea and Fire* show yet another magic world and yet another quest, both on a smaller scale than Tolkien's but so extraordinarily subtle and evocative that they have in a very short time achieved an enormous reputation among enthusiasts of epic fantasy.

E. E. Nesbit was a popular writer of children's stories in Edwardian England. Her tales of large families of imaginative children who became hopelessly and helplessly involved with magic creatures or things—a phoenix, a flying carpet, a magic ring—are still wonderfully readable today. Though never on epic scale, her works were revolutionary because they made use of absolute consistency—once the fantasy element was introduced, everything followed logically and no other fantastical things were brought in to solve matters. Tolkien and Lewis undoubtedly knew her work and were influenced by it. (As a matter of record, H. G. Wells did and was.)

Fletcher Pratt's *The Well of the Unicorn* was unique for its time. An extremely dense and detailed novel, definitely adult (particularly in its frankness about sexual matters), it appeared in the late '40s, and managed to thoroughly baffle everyone. Pratt describes the adventures of a young bumpkin in the feudal World of the Well. The magic, wizards, and trolls are simply aspects of that world, part of the background that only occasionally comes to the fore.

On the unspeakable side, there are several recent works that come so close to Tolkien as to evoke less polite words than "influenced by." I hope they will be conspicuous here by their absence.

And so, gentle readers, if you, like myself, are a hopeless addict of the incomparably strange and beautiful world of Professor Tolkien, there is no known cure. You can but blunt the hunger for more by collecting varied editions of his work, searching out other books that might approach his in enchantment, or, if worst comes to worst, try reading *The Hobbit* in Dutch.

No Monroe in Lothlorien

by Arthur R. Weir

Some books evoke pictures as we read them. How many of us, I wonder, have seen—clear before our mind's eye—the grim-faced Greys lined up for their last fight in *King Solomon's Mines,* or Edward Malone dropping his useless shotgun and using all his Rugby International's speed of foot for a desperate half mile down the moonlit avenue, with the great carnivorous dinosaur of *The Lost World* thundering behind him.

But of all books it is the collections of myths, legends, and fairy tales that are, in the most literal sense, picturesque; they draw their scenes, clear in detail and vivid in color and movement, before us as we read; and, as we reread them for the tenth or twentieth time, our familiarity with the text leaves us able to follow the print with but a small corner of our minds, freeing all the rest of our mentality to decorate and clarify the well-loved scene to something more real than any of the dull realities of every day.

One of the greatest of all these wonder provokers and image painters among modern books is J.R.R. Tolkien's *The Lord of the Rings* trilogy, and I think that most of us, in reading it, have found ourselves building in our imagination such a marvelous pageant of color, movement, action, and suspense as we had never hitherto dreamed might be evoked from us.

Given unlimited money and all the world's talent to command, how then would *we* set about turning it into the shadow reality of the silver screen of the cinema? This, surely, should be a labor of love for many minds to work upon, each contributing its best.

First, where and how are we to picture the fertile, well-farmed, kindly country of Hobbiton-in-the-Shire? The Yorkshire dales? The Cheshire levels, with their high ash hedges and black-and-white cagework farmhouses? The mile-wide fields of wheat or of gorgeous flowers of East Anglia and the Fen country? Or shall we follow Kipling's directions to "Lancaster County behind Philadelphia—a county of bursting fat fields, bursting fat barns, and bursting fat country girls—like what you might think Heaven would be like if they farmed there?" Or the snug, steep-sided valleys, hanging beechwoods, and orchard-bounded fields of the Cotswolds?

Then, at the other end of the scenic scale, what is to portray the grim evil of the Vale of Morgul with the wraith-haunted castle of Minas Morgul frowning at its end? The pitiless rocky desert of the Pass of Gorgoroth? The flaming ash-clad cliffs of Orodruin, the "Mount Doom" of the story's climax? Here again our choice is wide: the cliff-girt valley of grey rock and black rock with no single trace of growing green thing that was the scene of the famous Massacre of Glencoe; the endless miles of knife-edged lava clinker bristling with poison-thorned cactus of the Sonora Desert of Arizona; the iron-clad cliffs of the Sinai Desert springing vertically out of the desert sand, writhing and twisting and dancing in the heat haze that suddenly forms great sparkling lakes at their foot that equally suddenly shrivel and vanish; or, if we want something on the really grand scale, shall we go to where the Urumbaba Valley runs northwest from Lake Titicaca past the hidden Inca city of Machu Picchu—a narrow valley with sheer rock walls more than three-quarters of a mile high, of such terrifying appearance that even Pizarro's lion-hearted, iron-fisted soldiers crossed themselves uneasily when they first saw it, muttering to one another that this surely was the gate to Hell itself!

The castle of Minas Morgul has its own definite image in my mind—that of Schloss Thaurandt on the Moselle between Trier and Bonn, which was built in the middle of the fourteenth century by a genuine robber baron of most evil repute, and which retains to this day the marked impression of a construction built with no concession to any human requirement other than sheer defensive strength. Indeed, so well was this condition fulfilled that a force that outnumbered its defenders by fifty to one besieged it for over two years—and failed to take it!

Minas Tirith, the fortified city, with its seven great towers, sets another problem. Carcasonne is, of course, the ideal medieval city-fortress, but is so generally well-known to tourists that many in an average audience would immediately recognize it, spoiling the illusion. Another magnificently picturesque city is Jeysalmir in India, but that is set in bleak sandy desert, not the fertile fields of Tolkien's royal city.

The difficulty of finding suitable locations, however, are almost nothing compared with the difficulty of casting Tolkien's characters. With my own rather limited knowledge of film stars I can only think of two possibles: Alec Guiness as Gandalf, and

Charles Laughton as Theoden, the aging King of the Rohirrim. But who can we find to portray the combination of immense physical strength and fitness, many years of hardship and disappointment and yet essential underlying youth that is the long-awaited Prince, Aragorn? Even more difficult, how are we to portray Legolas the Elf, the deadly archer, the light-footed runner, who looks like a merry boy with a jest or song always on his lips, until a chance reference shows that he has, with his own eyes, witnessed events that took place some centuries before?

Most difficult of all, what are we to do about the Elf Queen, Galadriel? The very idea of any super mammary American or hip-waggling Italian film star in this part must fill the loyal Tolkien follower with sick horror! But the requirements are stringent—very considerable good looks, great natural dignity, the widest range of voice at all times under perfect control, the most graceful carriage and—on top of all this—the perfect naturalness that led to Sam Gamgee's artless tribute "And, with it all, she's as merry as any country lass a-dancing with flowers in her hair!"

It would have been an ideal part for Sybil Thorndike at her best; of all living film (or stage) actresses the only one I can think of who could—if she only *would*—take the part is Greta Garbo. This may, perhaps, raise the eyebrows of some, but not, I think, of those who remember her, as I do, in one of her last films, in which she played the part of a Soviet emissary to a western country, fanatically Communist, touchy, humorless, and suspicious. Towards the end of the

story an unexpected turn of events suddenly brings home to her the completely incongruous, wildly funny side of her own solemn pretensions and gives the picture of her I still love—Greta Garbo, lying back in her chair, laughing with all the artless happiness of a schoolgirl—rocking, gasping, finally weeping with helpless laughter—and all the audience at the film joining in from sheer delight!

Or would we need a ballerina to cope with the grace and dignity of motion that the part requires? Margot Fonteyn with a fairy makeup? Not Alicia Markova—neither her "refeened," best-behavior accent nor her kindly, unashamed London speech when at ease would fit such a part.

And, of course, Tin Pan Alley *would* try to introduce the latest hit tunes in the Halls of Elrond at Imladris! Luckily we have at hand one *genuine* piece of elf music in the shape of the strange haunting tune that appears in Kennedy-Frazer's *Songs of the Hebrides* under the name of "A Fairy Plaint" (music from inside a Fairy Hill). This is supposed to have been heard by a Benbecula crofter who, going home one night, found one of the fairy hills open, with lights inside and a crowd of elven-folk singing, harp-playing, and dancing. Scared nearly out of his wits, he hid behind a hillock and heard an elf harpist sing this song, which stayed in his mind—as well it might.

And now, with no financial considerations to worry about and all the world to choose from, who has some more good ideas for filming *The Lord of the Rings?* Let's hear them!

Goldberry

Christmas at the South Pole

by J.R. Christopher

"Well, my dears, there is lots more I should like to
say—about my Green Brother . . . ."
—*The Father Christmas Letters*

In the regions utmost southern,
on the continent Antarctic,
dwells one named for saintly Nich'las—
strange this Nicholas who dwells there.

Long his beard, and white and flowing;
ancient he and long enduring:
thousand years and more nine hundred—
soon (perhaps) two thousand reaching.

Green he chooses for his clothing—
green but trimmed with fur 'long edges,
warm enough for his June winters,
warm for his December summers.

There, beside the Pole most southern,
in his home with its four towers,
in his house there domed and shining,
in his cellared, storeroomed dwelling,

there, with penguins for his helpers—
emperors, Adelies also
(though the latter create trouble,
curious and nosy always)—

there, with elflings for his helpers,
packing gifts for those who write him,
packing them for those good children
in the hemisphere most southern,

from Angola through to Zamb'a,
Argentine, Brazil, and Chile,
Indonesia and Australia,
and Tahiti, and Samoa.

Once, when Amundsen came strolling
(that was back in nineteen 'leven),
or the twenty times the Goblins
have attacked the Southern Polar,

almost ev'rything went wrongly,
nearly missed deliv'ry's schedule,
but the Emperor of Penguins,
but the elven folk there working—

all together then averted
such catastrophe's occurence,
with their tricks or with their fighting—
stories worthy a full telling.

Now enough to sing of Nich'las,
Nicholas the polar ancient,
white his beard and green his clothing,
on Antarctica yet dwelling.

An Elven Brooch

A Baroque Memorial: J. R. R. Tolkien

by J. R. Christopher

Who is the stranger   staring at trees,
watching the oaks,   the elms admiring?
Whence has he come   to this curious forest,
this ancient woodland?   What welcome has found here?

The gnarled and twisted   trees so huge,
the man so small   he seems a halfling;
he stands amid roots   which rise to his knees.

Ovid and Seneca,   Statius, Claudian,
Nonnus and Chaucer   —the choice ones of old—
Spenser and Keats,   have spoken of trees,
have listed the species,   in lines of renown.
The HOLLY for peace,   pacem in terris,
is mentioned in song—   as a single bob;
the whitest flower,   the sharpest prickle,
the reddest berry,   the bitter bark—
the white for Christ's virtue,   the crown of its leaves,
the drupe red as blood   drained all so bitterly,
for the Torment of Christ was   on a Tau Cross,
shaped out of Holly,   Holly the holy one.
The FURZE, the gorse,   the fortunate shrub
(for shrubs also grow   green in clearings
in this ancient forest)—   the Furze with its spines,
its dark green branches,   its golden flowers

126

—frequented by bees,   the first of the year—
is burnt by shepherds   at the spring equinox,
for sheep to nibble   at the new growth,
burning, dying—   reborn like the Phoenix,
like Christ reborn.   The Quickbeam, the ROWAN,
the Mountain Ash,   is mentioned by Druids
for wands of wizards,   for of the wounded healing
(the Quickbeam will quicken   the quietest dying),
for calling on spirits,   compelling their answers;
the Rowan's red berries,   its red-berry clusters,
are the feast of dead heroes,   the food of the brave ones.

The HAZEL with filberts   is formed into thickets,
and wisdom is his   who wins to the center
to feed on the filberts,   to fill his deep longing,
to know the nine Hazels   nigh Connla's Well
which flower as they're nutting,   all fairness, all knowledge.

The YEW tree, the death tree,   the evergreen fadeless,
the longest-lived tree   in the lines of the poets,
whose branches make longbows,   whose berries make poison
(King Hamlet of Denmark   was harmed by the berry juice)—
the Yew tree has grown   in graveyards for ages,
with scarlet its berries   and scaly its bark,
and grown in the forest,   and flourished there ever.
The Aspen, WHITE POPLAR,   with silver-white leaves,
white bark on its branches,   bearing its catkins,
the tree of old age,   in Ireland was rod-shaped
to measure all corpses   and cunningly, mind them
that death was no end.   The ASH with its keys
was shaped once to wands,   wound with spirals—
by Druids was shaped thus   the shady branch-spreader;
was shaped once to   oars by ancients in Wales;
is shaped now to bats   for striking at baseballs—
how Ygdrasil's fallen,   the Ash of fame,
to popping up flies   in a popular pastime!
—but still in the forest   the shady one flourishes,
the tree of rebirth,   born from blood—
sacred and secret   the rites of rebirth.
These trees and these shrubs,   and several in addition,
are grown in this forest—   fir trees and oaks,
fruit trees, elms,   olives, palms;
the pine and the cedar,   the platan and cypress,
the willow and birch,   the beech and sallow,
the myrrh, the maple,   the myrtle, and more.

Amid those trees   are moving figures:
the lovers who've met   on a midsummer's night;
a duke who's led   his followers hence;
an army which is hidden   behind tree-branches,
so the wood seems moving; a steadfast maiden
from her younger brothers separated;
a poet who's heeding   a nightingale's song;
a leal band   in Lincoln green;
another poet whose passage is blocked
by a lion, a wolf,   and a leopard so gay—
almost, it seems   that Middle-earth
is but a forest,   a far-stretching woodland,
with stable cities   and civilizations
but clearings amid trees,   till the jungle takes them
like Mayan ruins,   like Olmec ruins—
Copán and Uxmal,   Vental and Albán.
(Have we killed the trees,   the corpses uprooted
with gigantic bulldozers,   the stumps and the stubs?
Have we destroyed the saplings,   till cities are cemented
with permanent boundaries,   unbroken forever?
Have we notched for extinction   that which Niggle painted?)

Deeper, deeper,   in the dark-shadowed forest,
which poets remember   and praise in their tellings,
as Joseph of Exeter   justly has catalogued
(and Statius and Claudian,   Spenser and Keats);
deeper, deeper,   in the darkened green glimmer,
where the great trees grow,   with grey lichens,
with tangled boughs   and matted twigs,
with ivy wrapped,   with cobwebs hung;
where sunlight's seldom—   a shaft in the shadows.
Deeper, deeper,   in the green darkness,
where the Onodrim dwell,   the tree-herding Ents
(ou sont les éspouses   of yesteryear?);
where the Elves on mellyrn   attach their telain,
the Quendi, first speakers,   questing for word-shapers;
where the White Tree grows,   seedling of Nimloth,
fruit of Galathilion,   descending from Telperion.
Deeper, deeper,   to the sacred center—
there is the stranger,   staring at trees,
watching the oaks,   the elms admiring;
gnarled and twisted   trees so high,
the man so small   he seems a halfling—
he stands amid roots   which rise to his knees.

There in the center   the sacred mound,
where once there were two,   two growing trees—
the one, an apple   (no holly at all,
whatever is claimed   in legends of old)—
the apple, which was cut,   was shaped to a cross;
the other, still growing,   still green and still thriving,
leaving and fruiting,   is the Tree of Life,
as was listed, yea catalogued,   by a poet of old.
And there is the stranger,   staring at trees;
he lifting a hand,   his right hand,
to the flourishing tree   picks a fruit:
the Fruit of Life   from the Tree of Life.

Sword Forged in Westernesse

The Crossroads

Two Poems in Memory of J. R. R. Tolkien

by Ruth Berman

I. Lament

Treeherd counted the depths of the wood.
Dryad, dryad, come back to the oak.
Treeherd wandered by river and hedge.
Nutmaid, nutmaid, turn in the hazel.
Treeherd circled the snowline, shivering.
Where are the greenhaired, blossomcrowned,
Angular maidens with barkbroken skin?
Treeherd wept like a tapped maple
For hamadryads nowhere to be seen
Twisted and beautiful, in the green shadows.

II. Firework's End

"'I hope you'll say a word about his fireworks,' said Sam."

Brief explosions of gold and green,
Coral branching into a moment's reef,
And a blue fan which, opening,
Is gone.
As each flares against the dark
It lights up the clouds of floating ash,
Immense, faint streaks of patchy light
Across the surface of deep heaven.
The moon drifts up, and as it clears the trees,
The wizard leans upon his staff
To put his squibs away.
Something he knows the moon knows, too.
The night grows cold.
Points of water gather into drops
And damp a wizard's cloak and hat.
Even wizards grow weary and long for bed.
The stars in the depth of the sky are bright
When the moon is down.

The Picnic:
A Parody of Tolkien

A Parody of Tolkien by Paulette Carroll

After an hour or so, the Company came to a small hill called Nemladrass in the Elfen tongue, and Doídrir in the dwarf language of Dane, that is, "small hill." There, Gandalf paused. "We must stop now," he said, "for our feet are weary and many miles lie still ahead of us. Who knows if we shall ever find a better spot in this dreary land?"

At these words, a shudder passed through the Company. "'Tis about time we halted, isn't it, my lad," said Sam, unloading Bill the pony. The poor beast looked at him as if it understood, as Sam lifted the picnic basket from its back. Gandalf quickly examined the contents, as the hobbits eagerly watched him, not daring to move. He seemed deeply absorbed in his thoughts, and a dreary silence fell on the Company. Finally, the wizard spoke. "The hour is grave," he said in a low voice. "This is much worse than anything I foresaw. The pickles are missing." "I didn't forget them, not me, Sir," said Sam defensively. "I thought of them all day long, and I wouldn't leave without pickles any more than without my master, bless me. I put them in the basket, didn't I, Bill, my lad?" The poor beast nodded, as if it understood. So did Gandalf. "Orcs took them perhaps," said Pippin. "I've always heard that they were fond of them."

Silence fell upon the Company. Even Bill seemed to avoid making a noise, as if it understood. The great shadow of the basket lengthened, and nobody dared touch anything. Straining his ears, Frodo thought he could hear the mournful growling of his stomach getting louder and louder. . . . Then Gandalf rose. "This is a wicked picnic indeed," he said, "since the pickles seem to be lost beyond any hope of recovery. But let us not despair. The onion rings are still here, and the Dark Lord shall not get them while we are alive. Let us eat."

And so they sat for hours, partaking of food, and the first bologna came to pass, and after it came many others. But still there was no sign of the pickles, or of what might have become of them. Nevertheless, their mood became gayer and gayer, and they sang old songs and told many a story, all at the same time and in different languages, none of which were still used at the time. Bill nodded, as if he understood.

Finally, Gandalf rose. "We must make haste," he said, "for already the sun is sinking in the west, and we have not yet reached dessert. The halflings are very slow to fill indeed. There is more to them than any of you realize."

The Coinage of Gondor and the Western Lands

by Dainis Bisenieks

INTRODUCTION. This brief history seems to derive from notes by Peregrin Took (as indeed does most of the lore of Gondor known to us). There are intimate references which must have come from him, but also there are additions by later hands. Since the days of King Elessar the study of coins has found a succession of devotees. At their hands this text has suffered abridgement and paraphrase and repeated translation, yet we must be grateful to have so much, for even the first who made himself a copy would not have had the coins. They suffered the fate of all the silver and gold that is not lost in the deeps or buried: to be worn down, melted, worked anew. In that way only do some of the treasures of Middle-earth survive today unless things buried chance to be found. In our gold coins and rings the gold of Gondor mingles with that of Egypt, Rome, the realm of the Aztecs, and the mines of California and Alaska.

Before the return of the King no Hobbit took much notice of the history of coins. Few indeed handled much money in their lives. Most gold and silver in the Shire reposed in household coffers and changed hands only when land was to be bought, or cattle or stores of goods. Accounts with tradesmen and innkeepers were tallied up and settled as the occasion arose. There was no authority to issue and regulate coin, and what money circulated was of the most diverse weight. Only in Bree could coins be tallied by count. Travelers from the outlands brought them: silver pennies which were made by all folk to the old Kings' weight, and other coin. But in S.R.

1422 came agents of the King with great wains to the Shire, bringing new coin in precious metal and bronze; and they bore away to his mints the gold and silver that the Hobbits exchanged for it. Scarce any hoard was not converted to King's money then. Now that there was small coin of guaranteed value, money came into common use, and workers in leather had to meet a sudden demand for purses.

There came to light then a diversity of coin such as no other land could have produced: scarce any less than a hundred years old, and many pieces worn smooth even with the scant handling they got: coins of Dwarves and Men and of the Kings of Arnor and Gondor that had passed away over a thousand years ago. The best of them, and others from hoards newly come to light, the moneyers sent to the King, who had them arrayed in glass cases in a room of the treasury. There all who desired might come and read on them the names of the kings who had reigned in the western lands for an Age of Middle-earth. Even coins of Elendil were there, which were then over three thousand years old.

What King in Elder Days first set his seal on gold and silver, no chronicle records, and none of their coins survive that might tell us. Númenor and all its treasures are sunk beneath the sea. The history of coinage must be chronicled from the coming of Elendil, though in his time it was already an ancient art. The men of other lands, in Rhun and Harad, all that had commerce with his realms, began in his day to strike coins after their standard. Some such may be seen in the King's treasury. Only their likeness of form and weight lets us guess at their history, since they bear no writing.

The kings of Gondor and Arnor had coins struck in both gold and silver; they bore as warranty of true weight the royal seal with the name of the king and the year of his reign. No change was made in that form while the lines of the Kings in North and South lasted; and both kingdoms kept ever the same standard of weight. It seems that no image was prescribed for the reverse of the coins, for no two of those that survive are alike. A man's purse in those days could serve for a picture book to ancient tales and scrolls of lore. None of the kings (save Castamir the Usurper) ever saw fit to vaunt their deeds or decrees by means of the coinage, which in our age was most notably done by the Romans.

Nor did any coin bear a portrait of the king, as they have done since Alexander the Great. What the practice was in the days of the glory and pride of Númenor cannot be known. Whether they did as the Númenoreans or the contrary, the kings of the Westlands were not portrayed on their coins, and a tradition came to weigh against such an innovation. It seems indeed a queer act of pride, for a king's face is scarcely ever noble and imposing above the ordinary run of men. Even if it were, artisans who had to cut new dies for every few thousand coins could not be expected to do it justice. So passed nigh on two thousand years of kings, and few are those whose features are known to posterity.

Mardil the Good Steward continued to issue coins in the name of King Earnur, and with the royal seal, but his successors used only the Tree as seal, and their coins read usually, "Of Gondor, under the authority [this formula came to be abbreviated] of the steward __," with the year of the Third Age. But in the years toward the final conflict, the seal was a city turreted and guarded: Minas Tirith, the Tower of Guard.

As a poem tells us, "There was an old dwarf in a dark cave, /To silver and gold his fingers clave;/ . . . and coins he made, and strings of rings. . . ." The dwarves did indeed coin both gold and silver, though not under the seal of any king. Their smiths would strike whatever coin was needed for commerce, and took great care that it be of true weight. Dwarvish money circulated widely in all the West and was eagerly sought after, for its beauty as well as its value. For dwarvish smiths adorned their work with many fair and curious devices, and scarce two coins might be found alike. A necklace of these was the pride of many a fair lady. Indeed, dwarvish coins were in origin rings and ornaments made to standard weights, but they grew accustomed to make them of the form and weight of the coins of the Kings.

When King Elessar took office, one of his first edicts was to have struck anew all the gold and silver in the coffers of Minas Tirith and all that passed in commerce through the city. In the course of only a few years all the coinage was renewed. His coins bore the White Tree in blossom with a crown above it and seven stars; they were inscribed, "Of Elessar, Isildur's heir, King of Gondor and Arnor." So his name and lineage were borne (as intended) into all corners of the world where the commerce of the kingdom passed, and few became the lands that had not heard of the King.

In celebration of the great victory, the coins bore for some years representations of the King's friends and allies and other tokens of the conflict that had passed. Riders of Rohan there were; an Elf with a bow; a Dwarf with an axe; a bear striking down a wolf, that was for the Beornings; a longship sailing up a broad river; and others besides. The Ents were not advertised to the world, which was as they wanted it, and neither were the Hobbits. The King thought long how he might represent them, but his friends made him see how untimely that would be.

Coins in bronze were issued, too, bearing images of birds and beasts. The largest, worth an eighth of the silver penny (which we must think of as equaling a drachma or a denarius), showed a mumak with a man on his back, flanked by two trees. For though these beasts had been the bane of many warriors, they were not evil in themselves, and the terror of the folk soon turned to wonder and pity. The coins were very popular in the Shire, but Sam found that nobody wanted to hear about oliphaunts any more.

Rohan now coined its own money, though coin of Gondor was current there too. Dwarves struck coins at need, as ever, but now many of their best artisans entered the service of King Elessar. Never had any prosperous realm, needing coins by the million, had so much fair and well-struck money. Dwarves worked, too, in the mints of Dale, whose small silver coins bore a thrush. Few Dalesmen knew

Erkenbrand of Westfold

why, though they loved their coins. Their largest coin was called a Daler.

After some years the King ordered the devices on his coins to be replaced by others less warlike. These were taken from ancient lore, but many events of the conflict recently ended were great matter for legend. A Hobbit first appears on the coinage in the guise of a gardener planting a tree, and for the Ents there was a tree root growing over an axe. No fierce bear, but a bee on a blossom now stands for the Beornings.

By a decree of the King many coins were struck every year showing the White Rider, Gandalf on Shadowfax; for Gandalf had now his place in the songs and tales of Gondor, as much as any hero of old. For all the years of the kingdom the heirs of Elessar continued the tradition.

In the last years of King Elessar appeared a coin showing two small figures, toiling up a mountain path. So were the Ringbearers at last made immortal, after the fashion of men, in gold. Indeed, gold may outlast the tales of men. It will, perhaps, shine brightly in the hand of one (man, or man's successor) who chances to find it a million years hence, and wonders what matter of legend were these small unassuming folk.

The Passing of the Elven-kind

A song in the mode *ann-thennath* by
Ted Johnstone

O'er all the lands the fair folk trod,
   The final eventide has come,
And those who wandered, silver-shod,
   Have faded from the changing land.
The march of man has pushed them from
   Their forest lands and verdant sod
Until at last they must succumb
   To forces they cannot withstand.

No more the fair Galadriel
   Will sing in green Lothlórien;
The empty halls of Rivendell,
   Deserted, silent, thick with dust,
Recall the empty hours when
   They stood as lonely citadel
Against the coming age of Men,
   But fell, as Elrond knew they must.

Lothlorien. A Maiden of the Eldar Race

The shadows of the fading age
  Grew long across the fields of gold;
The Elven-lords, each silent, sage,
  Had left the flow-ring mallorn trees.
For them the world was growing old—
  Though mankind saw a turning page—
The fair folk left their last freehold
  And passed beyond the Sundering Seas.

And Círdan wrought them ships which bore
  Them from the Havens o'er the sea
And watched them sail for fairer shore
  And leave the world of mortal man
In which no place for them could be.
  And in this world they stay no more,
But dwell in Elvenhome the Free,
  As fair as when the world began.

High Fly the Nazgul, Oh!

by Ted Johnstone and others

I'll sing you One, oh,
High fly the Nazgul, oh!
    What is your One, oh?
One for the One Ring, Lord of all, that was destroyed by Frodo.

I'll sing you Two, oh,
High fly the Nazgul, oh!
    What is your Two, oh?
Two, two, the watchful towers, guarding over Mordor, oh,
One for the One Ring, Lord of all, that was destroyed by Frodo.

I'll sing you Three, oh,
High fly the Nazgul, oh!
    What is your Three, oh?
Three, three, the Elf Rings,
Two, two, the watchful towers, guarding over Mordor, oh,
One for the One Ring, Lord of all, that was destroyed by Frodo.

I'll sing you Four, oh,
High fly the Nazgul, oh!
    What is your Four, oh?
Four for the Hobbits on the Quest,
Three, three, the Elf Rings,
Two, two the watchful towers, guarding over Mordor, oh,
One for the One Ring, Lord of all, that was destroyed by Frodo.

Nazgul

I'll sing you Five, oh,
High fly the Nazgul, oh!
    What is your Five, oh?
Five for the Wizards from the West,
And four for the questing Hobbits,
Three, three, the Elf Rings,
Two, two, the watchful towers, guarding over Mordor, oh,
One for the One Ring, Lord of all, that was destroyed by Frodo.

I'll sing you Six, oh,
High fly the Nazgul, oh!
    What is your Six, oh?
Six for the six names of the King,
Five for the Wizards from the West,
And four for the questing Hobbits,
Three, three, the Elf Rings,
Two, two, the watchful towers, guarding over Mordor, oh,
One for the One Ring, Lord of all, that was destroyed by Frodo.

I'll sing you Seven, oh,
High fly the Nazgul, oh!
    What is your Seven, oh?
Seven for the Dwarf-Lords' magic rings,
And six for the names of Strider,
Five for the Wizards from the West,
And four for the questing Hobbits,
Three, three, the Elf Rings,
Two, two, the watchful towers, guarding over Mordor, oh,
One for the One ring, Lord of all, that was destroyed by Frodo.

I'll sing you Eight, oh,
High fly the Nazgul, oh!
    What is your Eight, oh?
Eight for the swords of Westernesse,
Seven for the Dwarf-Lords' magic rings,
And six for the names of Strider,
Five for the Wizards from the West,
And four for the questing Hobbits,
Three, three, the Elf Rings,
Two, two, the watchful towers, guarding over Mordor, oh,
One for the One Ring, Lord of all, that was destroyed by Frodo.

I'll sing you Nine, oh,
High fly the Nazgul, oh!
    What is your Nine, oh?
Nine for the Walkers, questing bold,
And eight for the magic rune-swords,
Seven for the Dwarf-Lords' magic rings,
And six for the names of Strider,
Five for the Wizards from the West,
And four for the questing Hobbits,
Three, three, the Elf Rings,
Two, two, the watchful towers, guarding over Mordor, oh,
One for the One Ring, Lord of all, that was destroyed by Frodo.

I'll sing you Ten, oh,
High fly the Nazgul, oh!
      What is your Ten, oh?
Ten for the Battles of the Ring,
Nine for the Walkers, questing bold,
And eight for the magic rune-swords,
Seven for the Dwarf-Lords' magic rings,
And six for the names of Strider,
Five for the Wizards from the West,
And four for the questing Hobbits,
Three, three, the Elf Rings,
Two, two, the watchful towers, guarding over Mordor, oh,
One for the One Ring, Lord of all, that was destroyed by Frodo.
The Path to Mordor

Middle-earth

tune: "Penny Lane"   words: uncredited

In Middle-earth there is a tavern on the Eastern Road.
There travelers will find its tables full of cheer;
And when the innkeeper brings the beer,
He may bend an ear.

In Middle-earth well hidden deep in the Old Forest's trees
Tom Bombadil maintains a house of cobbled stone,
To which he brings Goldberry home
From the River's edge—to his bed.

Middle-earth beneath the Stars below the Sun,
Where the seedling of Telperion is planted;
  Elsewhere back

In Middle-earth there is a Hobbit in a hobbit-hole.
He keeps it clean although it's dug into the ground.
And though he spends a lot of time in town,
Still he's been around.

In Middle-earth there is a wizard with a staff of oak.
His flowing beard is colored like newfallen snow.
His fireworks light up the fields below,
And his smoke rings glow.

Middle-earth beneath the Stars below the Sun,
A wonder where the Norland waters run ere sunlight;
  Elsewhere back

In Middle-earth the wizard smokes his pipe contentedly.
We see the hobbits walking humming to the inn.
And then old Bombadil rushes in
From the River's edge—to his bed.

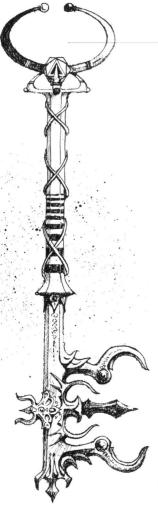

Key of Orthanc

Smaug the Magic Dragon

tune: "Puff the Magic Dragon"   words: uncredited

Smaug the magic dragon lived on the heath,
And in the lonely Mountain lay with treasure underneath.
Little Bilbo Baggins set off one summer day
With Gandalf and a bunch of dwarves to steal the gold away.
CHORUS: Smaug the magic dragon lived on the heath,
           And in the Lonely Mountain lay with treasure
             underneath.
           (twice)

The dwarves, when caught by goblins, escaped with Gandalf's aid,
And Bilbo found a magic ring that Gollum had mislaid.
They left the goblins puzzled, who thought it very weird
How thirteen dwarves, a wizard, and a hobbit disappeared.
CHORUS

They journeyed from the Forest; from the path they strayed.
They'd've all been spider-food without the hobbit's aid.
Escaping out of Mirkwood, the dwarves arrived in Dale,
Floating down the river cleverly disguised as kegs of ale.
CHORUS

They journeyed to the Mountain to find the dragon's store,
And Bilbo helped to find and open up a secret door.
The dwarves were all delighted when their burglar stole a cup,
But Bilbo wondered what would happen when old Smaug woke up.
CHORUS

The dragon, when awakened, was terribly perturbed,
Suspecting men of Laketown when he found his gold disturbed.
He flew with burning vengeance to leave the city charred,
But perished with his heart pierced by an arrow shot by Bard.
CHORUS

The Mountain King returned, the river flowed with gold,
And Mr. Baggins turned at last back toward his hobbit hole.
Returning from adventure, from war and dragon's lair,
He found Lobelia walking off with all his silverware.
CHORUS

The Orcs' Marching Song

translated by George Heap

tune: "Jesse James"

O, Sauron made some Rings, they were very useful things
And he only wanted One to keep
But Isildur took the One just to have a little fun.
Sauron's finger was inside it, what a creep!

CHORUS: Sauron had no friend to help him at the end
        Not even an Orc or a slave.
        It was dirty Frodo Baggins who fixed his little wagon
        And laid poor Sauron in his grave.

Now Sauron went to war for the glory of Mordor
But his Orcs didn't like the Sun.
Because marching in the heat made them feel so very beat
Sauron made them suntan lotion by the ton.

Gollum met his ruin while skin diving in Anduin
Where he found his birthday present.
He gave up steak and pork just to eat raw fish and Orc,
Though the flavor was unique, it wasn't pleasant.

Now the wizard Saruman heard that Rings were in demand
As a prelude to the arrival of the stork.
He decided Sauron's Ring would be just the perfect thing
For a wedding with a pregnant lady Orc.

Now when Frodo got the Ring he rather liked the thing
But it worried him every minute.
At the end of his long mission, to continue the tradition
He lost it with his finger still within it.

Sauron he felt poor at the fall of Barad-dur
And he didn't have a friend as I've mentioned
But his spirit lives today, just the same in every way
And the Orcs show up at every damn Convention.

Sauron is no more, and his land of Mordor
Was destroyed without any pity
But his spirit lives today, just the same in every way
On the House Un-American Activities Committee.

Shagrat's job went down the drain, at the end of Sauron's reign
And his new line of work is the result.
He's selling pornography, through the U.S.P.O.D.
And he prints it in a fanzine for the Cult.

Banner of Rohan

In the Service
of the King

by Marci Helms

News came slowly to the Shire even in those days, you know. Oh we heard rumors from the north. Rumors that Angmar, Witch-King was on the move again. Rumors that danger threatened the King. But rumors such as these had come before, in other years, and nothing had come of them. Usually they could be traced to some old Fallowhide who mumbled in his cups, or a Stoor whose fear of everything had for the moment focused on the creatures of evil which were said to follow Angmar. Yes, I remember the rumors. But that one winter was different. First, the rumors came, and we who thought ourselves wise, we who sat comfortably at home in the Shire, tending our pantries and gardens, dismissed these rumors too. But soon the rumors became news, news of Angmar's increasing power, news of his moves toward Arthedain.

I remember well the night I first believed that war had come again, the night I left the Shire. Lilly and I were there, sitting before the fire in the parlor. Lilly was embroidering a wreath of peonies on a new tea towel, and I was bent over my lap desk, writing a long letter to my uncle Arfogrim, talking mainly of the planting I had done that fall, and our plans to enlarge our smial, adding another pantry or two and pushing back the west wall of the kitchen. My mind was filled with the pleasant facts of life at home, life in the Shire.

I'd not thought anything amiss even when a loud knock sounded on the front door. Often my brother, Olo, or Lilly's sister, Floxie, and her husband Foldo, and their three littles would stop by for a chat about the fire, and they all, equally, knew that I meant to have a worker up from Hobbiton sometime to repair the bell. I thought perhaps in the spring, when the weather. . . .

Ah well, it wasn't for this that I started this tale . . . and thoughts of the quiet times at home hit too near the heart these days. You'll want to know about the war, and how we came to be here in this dead man's land.

It was Olo, alright, that night. He stood there wheezing and panting out the words. Words I hear now sometimes in the quiet of this cursed night that folds around me as I sit on guard duty— watching and waiting for those cursed orcs and the other misbegotten horrors to come out of the night to murder us.

"It's true, Folo. True. Angmar has Fornost. The King flees north. Angmar and his at his heels. The King has called for aid. . . . Some say Arveldul lies dead now, but I and others don't believe it. . . . But we're going north, tonight, the best archers of the Shire. The King needs us. Needs everyone against those demons. I came for you. . . ."

I stood before him, fear shaking my knees, but a swelling courage mounting within me. I went quietly about my home, gathering up this and that, fixing up a pack, selecting my best bow and three quivers of metal-tipped arrows, arrows that I'd used only for rabbits or crows. I didn't look at Lilly. She'd stood behind me there in the hall and heard Olo. I turned to her when he'd finished, but she only looked down at the tea cloth, twisted and torn in her trembling hands. She was crying, silently.

When I came again to Olo in the hall, Lilly had disappeared into the nearest pantry. I could hear jars and plates rumbling together and knew she was fixing a kit for me. "She sees the sense of it now," I thought, knowing that it was, in part at least, a lie. Olo spoke on and on, his words racing with his young enthusiasm. "We'll all be heroes," he said, and my heart half leapt to agree with him. Lilly returned, a well-stuffed basket under her arm. She gave it to me, and kissed me on the cheek. "I'll be home to see the roses bloom," I assured her as I went off down the path with Olo. She didn't speak, but a feeble smile pulled the corners of her lips up. She stood in the door and watched us go, the silence of leaving woven with the light of the hall candles wrapped about her shoulders. I think she mourned us even then.

We met the others before dawn at the Three Farthing Stone. At noon we turned east. It wasn't hard, marching along the east road. First we came to Frogmorton. One or two others joined us there. The children lined the roadway and cheered us on as they scuffled with each other, playing mock battles of hobbit archers against Angmar, and his hosts. Whitfurrows was the same, and so too was Bree, though more archers joined us there. The evenings were short. We marched til late, ate hurriedly from dwindling stores, and slept. We talked little, for the jests and jokes and hero boasts rang hollow against the chill of night and the fear that grew within us as we came nearer to the land of Angmar and his foul and vile minions.

We saw no one as we moved swiftly and silently towards Fornost. Perhaps we were too small and fast for the big ones to see. Perhaps we walked a lonely road.

One day a band of orcs fell upon us. Before we could nock arrows a third of our company lay dead, murdered by those vile-smelling creatures. We, the rest, killed them, all of them, I think. We shot arrow after arrow into their filthy bodies even after they'd died. We stood stunned. We stared at the orcs and our fellows, dead around us. Finally the moans of the few wounded brought us to action. Only Drolo, eldest of our company, had thought to bring bandages and healing herbs. How confident, or innocent, we'd been. We buried our dead, tended our wounded, and distastefully pulled our precious arrows from the carrion orcs.

A few days later a more wary party came just at dusk upon the lines of that foul dark horde. We moved more quietly than we had before, and came upon them, and feathered our way through a section before they even knew we walked among them. We left our arrows, that night, to show we, archers of the Shire, had come to the aid of our King.

One night we stayed within sight of Fornost's roofs, but dared not enter for we knew not if there were friends there yet. We feared that only wraiths and orcs lived there. Ours scouts went in and only one came back—only Olo. Olo had found a dirty, wounded man in a ruined cellar. He told Olo that all had left Fornost. All had gone north with the King. They hid in the old dwarf mines at the end of the mountains. The scouts had brought him most of the way out of Fornost before they'd been discovered by a patrol of Angmar's. The man and four of the scouts fell there; only Olo, he wounded in the shoulder, was left living to bring us this news. Our journey had not ended.

As light came, we were moving north again towards Forochel Bay. The days were short, the sun covered by clouds, the wind bitter, and none of our company knew the terrain. Our maps were vague and inaccurate. More and more, we began to travel at night. Our provisions were gone and we foraged. Some of our company took sick and two died. Others died in skirmishes with the enemy who, like us, prowled the mountains in search of the King. Once or twice we saw strange, fur-clad natives, but they spoke not our tongue. We hope to find the King soon. By day we search the mines and by night we oft huddle round the fires, our flesh and bones and souls are cold here. There are few enemies to kill now, perhaps the cold and hunger keep them from these passages. We hide from all, and from hiding strike and kill. We've grown practiced in it these many days.

Cold, on night's like this I wrap myself close in the cloak my missus wove, so long ago, and think of her and home. Is the Shire still as I remember it? Was it as glorious and peaceful as it seems now that I am far from it? Is the grass still green? The children still jolly? The times before the fire as good? I long for my pipe and weed, but the pipe was broken long ago in a skirmish—a delaying action really. And there is no pipeweed here in this place of death. Still, even were my pipe whole and my pouch full, I would not dare put fire to the bowl. The enemy have keen noses, and would thus smell me out, and so we would join the others who are colder this night even than we here about this cheerless blaze. The Shire, how I wish to be home. . . . But I fear for it, too. Has this menace reached its happy hills? How long can peace hold my homeland in her hand? How long can we little folk be sheltered? Do the others there live happy, never dreaming, even on the darkest night, of the terrors that hover round the boundaries of their land? I hope so. That thought would make it easier for me—this cold, this fight. But doubts will not be denied, and I wonder. Are they safe? Or do they suffer? Do they play? Laugh? Or are the biggest happenings of the year the careful but dull entries in the genealogies? Do they sit tear-faced and mourn us? Do they know that we are gone? Do they remember us? Oh Lilly, do you, this night, remember me?

It is said in Appendix A, part iii, of *The Lord of The Rings* by J.R.R. Tolkien that "To the help of the King they (the Shire) sent some archers who never returned. . . ."

Faramir's Vision

Haiku Portraits

by
Don Studebaker,
Ted Johnstone
and others

Moon-silver beauty;
Soft song bringing ancient tears
To the elven-lords.
—Lúthien Tinuviel

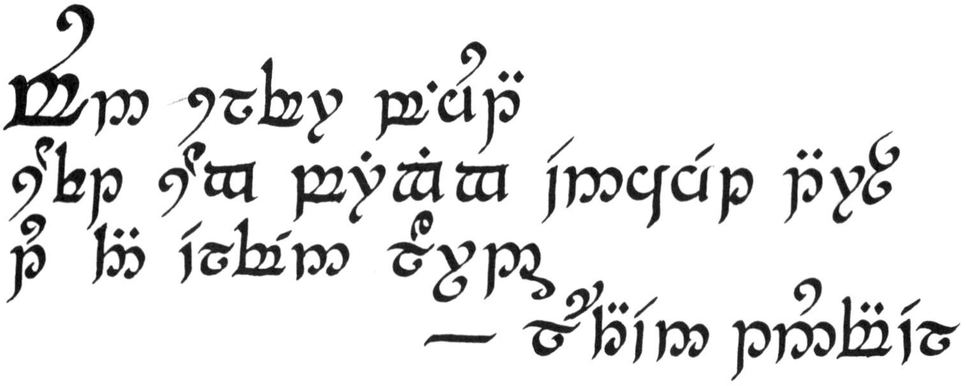

Darkness wore a cloak;
Wrapping for a pale rider
Astride a black horse.
—Nazgul

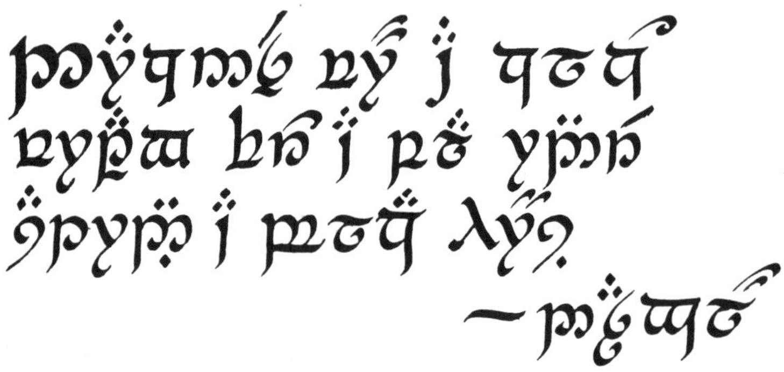

Beneath the black crown;
Red, in a skull of blue fire,
The Eye burns with hate.
      —Sauron

Snowy brows, blue eyes;
A flash of fire and thunder—
The old grey pilgrim.
      —Gandalf

Tall, straight, leather-hard;
Blood of past and future kings,
With a broken sword.
      —Aragorn

Tales Told by the Lonely Mountain

by Margaret M. Howes

These legends of the time of the Northmen were told in Lake-town, and later in the restored kingdom of Dale, where they were finally put into writing during the reign of King Elessar.

It is most unlikely that any of them can be accepted as historical, even the tale that purports to tell of the downfall of the great king Bladorthin. His name, of course, is historical, being mentioned in Bilbo Baggins' narrative, *There and Back Again*; the spears intended for his armies, never delivered or paid for, still lie in the treasury of the King under the Mountain. Nevertheless, we do not know for sure that he was even a king of the Northmen; most authorities are of the opinion that he was a king or ruler of elves.

However, these stories undoubtedly do show something of the quality and style of life that must have existed among the Northmen of the lands around Erebor in the days before the coming of Smaug; a life more savage and brutal than that of Gondor, even in its waning days, among a people who had had little or no contact with the civilizing influences of either Dúnedain or elves.

THE FALL OF BLADORTHIN

Bladorthin was a great king, descended from Bladorn, the dragon slayer. Bladorn it was made himself high king over all the kings of the Northmen, and made Erannan of his mother's people the greatest and most powerful in all the northern lands.

In the time of Bladorthin was plenty: grain in the fields, fish in the rivers, mast in the forests. Every cow brought forth twins, and every man dwelt at peace with his neighbor. The war band went out to the north against the goblins of the mountains, and south against the enemies of the king. Every man wore gold and silver, and every woman silk. Wine of Dorwinion came up the river to the men of the northern lands.

There was a lord named Ruand, king of the fort of Slimen. He it was raised rebellion against Bladorthin, and destroyed the peace of the land. For Bladorn had many sons and daughters, and many of the chiefs could claim descent from him. And this was rebellion, for Bladorn himself desired the high kingship should go to them of Erannan. He it was that gave the high kingship to his own son, Madan, there in Erannan, and Madan to his son Blad, and Blad to Bladorthin.

Now a man came from Slimen, Atan by name, secretly to the king. He told of the devices of Ruand, and of the chiefs and lesser kings who were leaguing themselves with Ruand.

Bladorthin was loth to believe this, or to move against his own kinsmen, unless they should openly take up arms against him. But he increased his own war band, and sent to those chiefs whom Atan had named loyal, asking them to name those who could bear arms in his service if need should rise. These chiefs sent back the word, that such and such a number would be sent, in that case.

Bladorthin then sent a herald and messenger to the King under the Mountain to bargain for swords, mail, and especially spears, the finest of all these things that could be made, to equip all those men who might be serving him. The bargain was struck, and the anvils of the dwarves rang day and night, forging such arms as had not been seen before in those lands.

Mail they had, and swords; but the spears had not been delivered before Ruand and his allies, and all their war bands, fell upon Erannan in a single night, and by surprise they overcame. They came in the dark of the moon, and the sentries gave no warning, for it is said they had been bribed by Ruand with promises of rich lands of their own if they should aid him.

Ruand and his men they surrounded Erannan and threw up great ladders and swarmed in the thousands over and into the forest, leaping down from the walls full armed. Erannan, greatest of strongholds was put to the torch and the sword. The women were ravished, those that did not thrust the knives to their own hearts; the children dashed against the walls. Bladorthin and his sons died fighting, and a heap of bodies of the slain men of Ruand walled them round when at last they fell.

Now Atan had fought near the king and his sons (for he was himself kin to Bladorthin) and strove to cut his way to them through the press. But when he saw them fall and knew all were dead, he forced his way out of the fight and came to the inner chamber. There was the queen lying in her blood, she being one of those who took their own lives for fear of greater shame. Now the youngest child of the king, his daughter Muirne, was in the arms of her old nurse, and sobbing with terror were both of them.

Now Atan hushed the woman, and the woman hushed the child; and he was in a frenzy to get them safely out of the fort. There was a little door and a passage there that led out to the midden heap, where the servants had tossed the slops; and he found rags and put them over his armor, and threw aside his sword, keeping only a long knife concealed under his rags. He wrapped the woman and the child in rags, and, he carrying the princess, they crawled half on their bellies out the little passage.

He left them by the midden heap, the old woman shivering and huddling with fear, clutching the child under her rags and crouching against the reeking heap.

Now Ruand's men and those of the other chiefs were fighting no longer, but carousing and shouting, drinking up all the king's store of wine as they looted the fort. Atan moved quiet and careful

out of their sight and found six other men at arms surviving from the king's guard. When night had fallen they gathered, rags over their armor, and with Atan they carried the princess Muirne and her old nurse out of the fort. The gates were open and no sentries posted, for the dead queen had been found and Ruand was sure he had done for all of Bladorthin's family and his heirs.

They went north throughout the night, and when dawn came they sheltered in a little scrubby wood. It was high summer and there was plenty of cover, and they were grateful for that. There was water, and they had bread to feed the princess, but no more. At night again they moved on, and took shelter again by day, for Ruand's men were roving about the lands.

So they travelled, and zigzagging they made their way westward toward the Lonely Mountain, where the town of Dale and its king stood secure. Rabbits and squirrels they caught, and cooked on tiny fires, and careful they were lest they show any smoke. Sometimes they went hungry, but they kept the princess alive.

And at last they rounded the eastern spur of the Lonely Mountain, Erebor, and saw the merry town of Dale before them. The gates

The Palantir

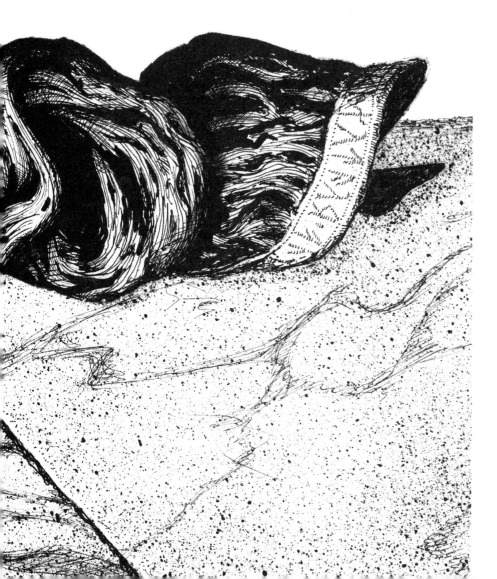

of Dale stood open, for they feared no enemy in their hold against the mountain, and they were allies of Thror, the mountain king.

Then Atan and the others came like beggars to the gate of king Ornin, and sat down beside it; and Atan told the gateman he was a bard of great gifts, escaped from the ruin of Erannan, and begged to see the king. The gateman left, and soon returned, and Atan was led before the king. There he revealed himself, and showed to the king the seal of Baldorthin, which his infant daughter had worn around her neck.

"We have heard indeed of the fall of Erannan," King Ornin said. "Sorrow it is that such a stronghold should be destroyed, that has stood as long as memory! But best we say nothing of the lineage of the princess. Let my own wife take her as foster child, and let none know of her parentage."

So he sent a messenger, saying, "Let those ragged supplicants at the gate be granted entry, and the innocent child with them, for they shall be granted the mercy of the king."

So it was done. And the queen came also, with young Girion, her only son, and took the infant princess into her arms as fosterling and the old nurse was kept to care for her.

And Atan and the men served King Ornin in his guard. But the word was given out that all of them, including the child, were mere penniless wanderers, the men homeless fighters, and that all that was done for them was simply of the mercy of the king.

Now Ruand was thinking to make himself high king in place of Bladorthin. But his own allies said to him, "Who are you to set yourself above us? We too are of the line of Bladorn, and it's not we who will bow the knee before you! As equals we fought and as equals we will reign, each man in his own place, and let you be sharing out equally the booty of the taking of Erannan, or take it we will ourselves!"

So the treasure of Erannan was shared out, whether Ruand would or no, and they returned to their own forts. Then Ruand strove to refortify Erannan, and little it was he had done when those men who would have aided King Bladorthin now gathered to avenge him, and they came down on Erannan and now Ruand fell, and the fire raged again through Erannan and left it in ruins altogether. Then those who had fought with Ruand rose up against the avengers of Bladorthin, lest they share Ruand's fate, and so the fighting raged, now around one fort and again around another, and not one willing to speak the word of peace.

There was no end. Woman, child, aged man, or crone were not spared. None were left to till the soil, and famine was on the land. Avengers and rebels all alike were become robbers and reivers, for not one but could claim himself in somewhat an heir of Bladorn's line, and not one who did not dispute the claim of all the others.

So those who tired of rapine went to take service under King Ornin, and pledged themselves to him. He gave them lands to till, or service among his warriors, and his own realm he extended far south and east of Esgaroth, and many were its people.

Now Muirne had grown to womanhood, and fairest in Dale she was. At this time, then, her parentage was revealed, and with great ceremony she was wed to Girion, heir of Dale. Great joy was in all the lands around, and the remnants of the Northmen came eagerly to Dale.

When Girion became king his realm was far greater than his father's, and again there was peace and plenty in the land. In due time a son was born, and he was named Bladorn, for the hero of old, and in him men said there would be restoral of the high kingship. For his arming when he came of age, he was clad all in mail of the dwarf-forging, and Girion gave to Thror, the dwarf king, a necklace of emeralds from faroff Rhun, each one as big as a man's two fists. Rich was Dale, and rich was Esgaroth; the bells rang merrily, and joy was there.

Then the dragon came to Erebor.

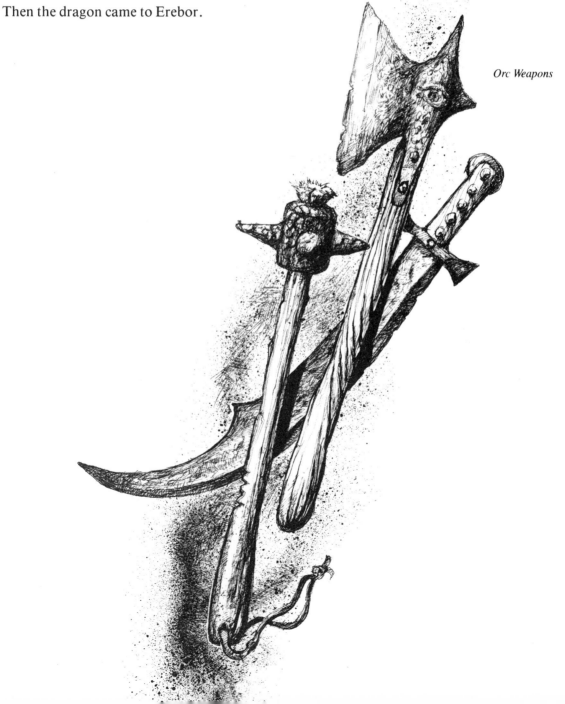

Orc Weapons

THE STORY OF BREGA, SON OF NAR

There was a warrior named Brega, son of Nár. His father's father's brother had been king in Niping, and he and his family had been put down by the men of Narod; now Brega was only a man of arms of the fort, and this was a shame to him. He went away from Niping to dwell in the eaves of Mirkwood, and there he was joined by many, outlaws and masterless men, their hands against everyone, living however they might.

Brega's heart grew hot within him when he thought that his line had once been kings. He thought first of Niping, but his thought grew ever higher until at last he thought of Erannan, greatest of forts, with all its riches. Then he called together the band of his followers and spoke to them. "We have no heroes' portions in any fort. Let us go up against Erannan, greatest of all, and stand or fall by the might of our arms."

So they went up against Erannan. They broke through the gate and fired the king's house and his four sons within it, but then they were surrounded by them of Erannan, and overcome. They were dragged before King Madan, and full of grief and rage he was. "For my house I take nothing; but for my sons a worthy weregild I will have, or your lives in the getting of it."

Brega said wearily, "These are our fortunes, then. What is this weregild you will have?"

"I will have the crown of the king of Dorwinion, and it taken from his head as he sits in his council in the highest castle of Dorwinion, and this I lay on you: you will have no rest in any of the lands of men, until my weregild is won."

So Brega and his men went down to the Long Lake, and they seized a ship from a merchant of Esgaroth. "If we achieve our weregild, and come back from Dorwinion," said Brega, "it's plenty of gold we're likely to have as well, and the fat merchant will have his pay. If we come not back, let him send for the ship, and see what Erannan or Dorwinion will do for him." For Brega was a rough, hard-spoken man, and his following like to him; and they thought they might be going to their deaths, in any case.

So they sailed for many a day, for the river runs long down to the Sea of Rhun. It grew much wider, and there were fat orchards and fields of grain on either side, and red cattle in the meadows. Then they took care and rowed along at night, their sails all lowered, and laid themselves up for the days under the banks of reeds and sedges that grew along the river.

At last they could see the hills of Dorwinion rising in the distance, covered with vines, and they heard the gulls of the sea crying high, and then they took thought to how they were going to achieve that crown.

"Shall we be hiring ourselves to the king as soldiers?" said one. "Then surely we will be finding our chance to seize the crown."

"Well said," answered Brega. "Do we be sailing up in good order and all open, and offering ourselves to serve in his guard; and serve you faithfully and well and say nothing of the crown, until the time that I say, 'take!' Then he who stands nearest the king will seize that crown, and it's down to the river we'll be and into the boat and away. And have your swords ready to be cutting our path.''

So it was agreed. They sailed openly into the town, with the vines making the land green all around, and on top the highest hill the castle of the king. They marched up and entered the hall, and there sat the king, but no crown on his head, only a cap of velvet and fur. And on each side of his throne crouched a great ugly goblin.

Brega and his men said nothing about it, but struck their bargain to serve the king, which was easy enough, for they were fine men a half head taller than them of Dorwinion. Now the Northmen were two hundred in number.

As they went to the place where the guard were housed, Brega said to the captain, "It's an odd crown your king is wearing, and odder sorts of dogs he has by his heels."

"That is not his crown," said the captain. "His crown is the richest in Middle-earth, of silver overlaid with gold and that overlaid with mithril, come from the dwarves of Moria long ago; and that studded with diamonds, rubies, emeralds, pearls, and all other jewels, and a cap beneath of velvet, hung with other gems and broidered with thread of gold. On a single day of the year in high council he wears it, and the men of his guard with drawn swords around him, and two others to hold up the weight of it as it rests on his head. And the goblins are indeed his dogs, as you have seen, slaves to his family from the time they began to be kings. And there have been a hundred kings in Dorwinion, and those same two goblins serving them. And those two goblins are knowing the smell of every particular man about the king, and yours as well already, and will be tracking down an evildoer though he should swim the Sea of Rhun.''

Then Brega and his men understood the vengeance of King Madan, and despair was in them. But they said nothing and served the king all that year. And it was a true word King Madan had when he said they would have no rest in any of the lands of men, for Dorwinion was a rich prize and always its men were fighting the Easterlings and other wild tribes, and Brega and his men were always killing twenty to every one man killed by them of Dorwinion, but still eighteen of them got their death that way.

Then the year was up, and the king held his high council again. All his nobles were there, and the men of his fiefs; and he entered the hall in cloth of gold. Two men in cloth of silver bore up his crown, with the rays of it glittering like the sun throughout the hall. The two goblins came crouching beside him, more hideous than ever, as he seated himself upon his throne.

Now all the guard, and Brega and his men among them, stood round with drawn swords. Then at last Brega cried, "Take!" and himself he snatched the crown from the king's head, and then the Northmen drew all together and cut their way out of the hall with such a slaughter as had never been seen in Dorwinion, and down to the docks and into their boat. But they left twelve dead behind them, and the goblins were at their heels.

So they rowed up the river all day and all night, until their backs and their arms were cracking, and they pulled ashore at last in the dark of night. There was a war band waiting for them, that had ridden hard following the goblins. A great fight they had on the shore and cut down the men of Dorwinion, and most of all they were trying to get at the goblins, but those fled into the dark when the fight began.

So they got no rest that night, and five more behind them they left dead, and it was back to the boat again.

Up the river they went, half of them rowing at a time and the other half resting on their oars, for they knew they would be getting no rest on shore. Raw fish they ate that they caught as they went, and ten more of them died of their wounds and the rowing, and they cast them in the water and rowed on.

They came to Rivers Meet, and there they pulled out on shore. For some days they had seen no riders or goblin shapes along the banks, and they thought they might be safe. Two nights they rested, and on the third they were attacked. Them of Dorwinion were now on foot, and the last of the bands sent north. They had ridden their horses to founder them and the goblins had sniffed the way and now with all their might they came on Brega and his men. Like lions the Northmen fought until the others were dead or fleeing away with weariness. Then they went back to the boat, but the goblins had been at it, and stove it in.

So they took cobwebs, and stuffed them in their wounds, and they ran then, north from Rivers Meet. And the men of Dorwinion pursued, and ever and again they caught up and there would be hard fighting; and always more dead of Dorwinion than of the north there were, but always some left to come behind. And the goblins kept the pursuit, and never within swords' reach did they come.

At last there were none of Dorwinion left, and only the goblins following, and Brega and two of his men remained, and half dead of wounds and weariness they were, but still they bore the crown. They came past the Long Lake, and in the dusk they saw the lights of Esgaroth across the water. Then in the dimness beside the lake, the goblins leaped upon Brega's men, with great claws and mighty tusks tearing them to pieces.

Now Brega in a terrible rage sprang up, and swung his sword like a lightning flash, and hewed those goblins into chunks and gobbets, the dark blood spouting around. And from the very force of his wrath, his own wounds burst out again.

Now that night there was merriment in the hall of Erannan, for it was a festival time. The king lounged at ease at the head of the hall, and his men and their wives and maidens at the long tables on each side. Torches burned in the cressets, and the harpers harped, and a juggler performed his antics before the king.

One came in saying that a lone man craved entrance to the fort and the hall, and the king granted it, saying no man would be refused that night.

So the door opened, and a man staggered in. Half naked he was, and filthy rags hung about him; his beard and hair sticking out like straws and his eyes wild; blood was clotted on his wounds and fresh blood flowed, and he fell on the floor and something rolled from his hand to the feet of the king.

Silence there was in the hall, and the king picked the thing up, and stared at it in wonder, and then lifted it high, crying out, "The crown of Dorwinion!" And a great shout went up that shook the hall.

Then someone turned over the body of the man on the floor, and he was dead, and they saw that it was Brega, son of Nar.

THE VENGEANCE OF ANDOR

There was a king in Niping, and Torna was his name. He had a wife, the daughter of the king in Cuala, and a fine son she had borne him; but he set his love on a woman of his own clansmen. Besotted he was, and nothing would do but he must have this woman, and his true wife and their son he sent back to Cuala.

Furious was the king in Cuala, and would have made war on Niping. But his daughter said, "Let you be waiting until my son is grown." For she was a wise woman. So they waited, and the time passed by. Each night as her son, Andor, lay sleeping, the queen would sing strange spells above his cradle. Also as he grew, he learned the use of sword and spear, but more than any of these he studied the wisdom and the magic of his mother.

So the years went, and more and more it was said that not Torna, but Esig, his mistress, ruled in Niping.

One day one came to Niping an enchanter he was of power. Many strange works of magic he performed, and the words of beasts and birds he understood, and it was said that he could prophesy the future.

The woman, Esig, sent for him.

"What can you tell me of the years to come?" she asked.

"Filled with power are the years to come," he told her.

"Power for whom?" she asked.

"Power for those who can hold it," he said. "A great king is not content with a little land. To the east are many hills, and filled with wealth they are. Should men leave the greatest bounty to those who are but half men?"

Now it was the dwarves of the Iron Hills he spoke of, and Esig knew this well. No man had ever sought to seize their lands and the great hills that were bored through and through with their mines and tunnels and passageways, smoking always with the fires of their forges. But now Esig began to speak of this to the king, and of the great wealth of the dwarves hidden in the earth. Ever and again she sent for the enchanter with his harp, and soon the king was listening also.

Then King Torna desired the lordship of the Iron Hills, as he had desired the woman, Esig, and he began to arm his men to march to the hills. It was a madness on the men of Niping, and the enchanter moved among them and spoke of power to come; and ever and again he struck his harp and sang a mighty lay of the heroes of old.

On a day in spring they marched out then, all the fighting men of Niping, save for a little force of old men and boys left behind to guard the walls. They sang as they marched eastward, King Torna and the woman Esig marching together at their head, both in arms. The enchanter was following, with his staff and his harp.

Now the dwarves are fearsome fighters. Short they are in stature, but broad and mighty in strength, and a terror when they defend their own. They wear steel mesh down to their knees, more heavy than a man could bear, and use sword, spear, and battle axe as if they were child's toys, made of lath.

Far off on the plain they saw the men of Niping coming, and out of the hills they poured in the thousands, ready for the fight.

Terrible that battle was. The men of Niping were maddened with the battle rage, and fought they did until they fell where they stood. As for the dwarves, they gave not one step back and there before the Iron Hills they cut down Torna's army.

Now one man lived, and sought to find the bodies of King Torna and of Esig. It was the enchanter, and in time he found them, dead together on the field.

Then came the dwarf king, Dain; he said to the living man, "What do you here? Is it so eager you are for the fate of all these others?"

"I have borne no arms against you," said the man, and showed that he bore only harp and staff. "I would not quarrel with those who hold in right the Iron Hills. I ask your grace only to return to Cuala, my own place."

"Go, then," said the dwarf king. "Go and tell them what happened on this field, and give them warning henceforth to keep their quarrels among themselves."

"I'll do that," said the man. "And my thanks and my gratitude go with you, in farewell."

So the dwarves marched back into the Iron Hills.

Now the enchanter started for Cuala, but when he was far out of sight of the hills, he turned aside to a little hidden hollow. He threw aside his gray enchanter's robe and bathed in a small pool there, and when he emerged, it could be seen he was a fine, strong, handsome man, in truth like to them of Cuala. He dressed as a prince should dress, then, taking clothing, armor, and weapons from a small cave behind a rock; then he went striding on his way towards Niping.

He came to Niping, and rapped on the gate with his sword hilt, and they let him in; and he told them of the battle before the Iron Hills. Now when they had finished their weeping and bitter mourning, they asked him who he was.

"I come from Cuala," he said, "and I am Andor, son of Torna. My father and the woman, Esig, I found dead, there on the battlefield. Who now will you have as king in Niping?"

And with one voice they cried that Andor should be king.

So he reigned, and there was peace in Niping in his time, and after a while he brought warriors from Cuala, from his mother's brother, who was now Cuala's king. These were young warriors, well-favored men, and many a widow in Niping was glad to wed again, and so Niping lived. Andor's mother he brought back to Niping as well, and she lived there and was held in great honor all her days.

Typical Sheriff of the Shire

The Middle-earth Gourmet

by Maureen Bayha and Alida Becker

There's almost nothing a hobbit loves quite so much as a good meal—unless it's an unexpected, extra meal. Civilized life in the Shire revolves around "plenty of food at regular and frequent intervals," and the pantries of hobbit *smials* are stocked with enough delicacies so that no opportunity for feasting needs to be missed. A hobbit larder can produce, on a moment's notice, the makings of a high tea or a family picnic, or even provisions for a journey to Erebor.

Proper hobbit food is rather simple and hearty, much like English country fare. Although the dish hobbits talk of most often is a simple breakfast of fried eggs and bacon, they're certainly not willing to slight the other meals on their daily schedule. Any time of day, hobbits are always interested in "something hot out of the pot," and if that something is liberally laced with mushrooms, so much the better.

In fairness, though, we must remember that other denizens of Middle-earth have to get by with a bite now and then, so our collection of recipes includes a bit of "fissh" for Gollum, a leg of mutton for a troll, and seedcake for the dwarves. Alas, the food of the elves cannot be duplicated by other Middle-earth cooks; and as for that of the orcs, who'd want to?

Frodo's Scones

In a large bowl, sift together 2 cups of sifted all-purpose flour, ½ teaspoon of salt, ½ teaspoon of baking powder, and 1 tablespoon of sugar. Cut in ½ cup of shortening. Add 1 cup of raisins or currants. Make a well and add enough buttermilk to form a stiff dough. Roll out ¼ to ½ inch thick on a floured board. Fry on a lightly greased griddle for 7 to 10 minutes. Turn. Fry for 7 to 10 minutes more and serve.

Bilbo's Orange Marmalade

Wash, dry, and peel 2 pounds of smooth, unblemished oranges. Cover the peel with cold water and simmer for 2 hours, until it is tender. Slice the oranges very thin and mix with 2 pounds of sugar. Drain the peel, cool, and scrape out the white pith. Slice the peel very thin. Combine the oranges and peel, and stir well. Simmer over a low heat until thick. Pour into hot, sterilized jars and cover.

Smaug's Gems

Combine 1 cup of vanilla wafer crumbs, 1 cup of confectioners' sugar, 1 cup of chopped nuts, and 1 tablespoon of cocoa. Add 2 tablespoons of light corn syrup and ¼ cup of whisky. Mix well and shape into 1 inch balls. Roll in confectioners' sugar and place in an air-tight container. Store in the refrigerator.

Fruit Fool à la Sackville-Baggins

Cook a quart of berries (gooseberries, raspberries, or blackberries) in a heavy saucepan over a low heat for 30 minutes, stirring and mashing constantly. Add 1 cup of sugar and simmer until the sugar is dissolved. Purée in a fine sieve, cover, and refrigerate. Just before serving, whip 3 cups of heavy cream and fold it into the fruit mixture. Serve at once.

Merry's Mulled Cider

Mix together 2 quarts of apple cider, 20 whole cloves, ½ cup of sugar, 12 sticks of cinnamon, 14 whole allspice, and ½ teaspoon of salt. Bring to a boil. Simmer for 15 minutes. Keep warm. Strain and serve in a mug with a lemon slice.

Mrs. Maggot's Cottage Pie

Slice a large onion and 2 carrots and sauté in bacon fat until the onions are limp. Add 1 pound of cubed beef, 1 tablespoon of flour, and salt and pepper to taste. Sauté for several minutes, then add ½ cup of beef stock and simmer for 20 to 30 minutes. Peel and quarter 1 pound of potatoes and boil until soft. Mash with 2 to 3 tablespoons of butter and enough milk to make a soft mash. Season with salt and pepper. Put the meat in a pie dish, cover with the mashed potatoes, and bake in a 375 degree oven for 30 minutes. Before serving, run the dish quickly under the broiler to brown the potato crust.

Mushroom Soup from the Inn at Bree

Chop ½ pound of mushrooms very fine. In a large saucepan, melt 4 tablespoons of butter. Add 1 tablespoon of chopped onion, 2 cups of finely chopped carrots, 2 cups of finely chopped celery, and 1 clove of garlic, minced. Stir in 2½ cups of beef broth, 3½ cups of water, 1 small can of tomato paste, ¼ teaspoon of salt, and ¹⁄₁₆ teaspoon of pepper. Bring to a boil. Cover and reduce heat. Simmer 1 hour. Purée the soup. Melt 2 tablespoons of butter in a skillet, add ½ pound of sliced mushrooms, and sauté for 5 minutes. Add to the soup. Add ¼ cup of dry sherry. Heat thoroughly and serve.

Mirkwood Cookies

Sift together 2½ cups of flour, 2 teaspoons of double acting baking powder, and ½ teaspoon of salt. Cream ¾ cup of butter. Gradually add 1 cup of brown sugar (granulated brown sugar works well), creaming well. Blend in 1 unbeaten egg and 1 teaspoon of vanilla and beat well. Melt 1½ squares (1½ ounces) of unsweetened chocolate; set aside to cool. Add the dry ingredients gradually to the egg mixture. Mix thoroughly. Remove ⅔ of the dough to a floured pastry board. Stir ¼ teaspoon of baking soda into the chocolate. Blend the chocolate mixture into the remaining ⅓ of the dough. Chill if necessary for easier handling. Roll half of the light-colored dough into a 10 by 4 inch rectangle. Shape half of the dark (chocolate) dough into a 10 inch roll and place on the rectangle of light dough. Mold the light dough around the dark dough and wrap in foil. Repeat with the remaining dough. Chill for at least 2 hours. Cut the dough into slices ⅛ to ¼ inch thick. Place 2 slices together on a greased cookie sheet to resemble eyes. Pinch the corner of each slice to give a slant-eyed look to the cookie. Place a chocolate chip into the center of each eye. Bake for 8 to 12 minutes in a preheated 350 degree oven. Remove from the baking sheets at once. Store between layers of foil in a flat, covered container. Makes approximately 3½ dozen cookies.

Beorn's Honey Nut Cake

Put 1½ cups of cottage cheese through a strainer. Mix the strained cottage cheese with 1½ tablespoons of sifted flour, ¼ teaspoon of salt, 3 tablespoons of sour cream, 3 beaten egg yolks, ¾ cup of honey, 1 tablespoon of butter, 1 tablespoon of lemon juice, the rind of 1 lemon, and ½ cup of wheat germ. Fold in 3 egg whites, stiffly beaten. Butter a 9 inch square cake pan. Sprinkle the bottom of the pan with ⅛ cup of wheat germ. Pour the batter into the pan and top with ⅛ cup of wheat germ and ½ cup of chopped nuts. Bake in a preheated 375 degree oven for 30 minutes.

Scotch Eggs Strider

Hard boil 8 eggs. Cool and peel. Mix together 1 pound of sausage meat, ½ teaspoon of sage, 1 tablespoon of parsley, and a pinch of thyme (or use 1 pound of sage-flavored sausage). With the sausage meat make 8 patties large enough to surround the 8 peeled, hard-cooked eggs. Place an egg in the center of each patty and form the sausage around the egg. Roll the egg in flour seasoned with salt and pepper, then in beaten egg, and then in bread crumbs. Fry in deep fat.

Baked Bluefish For Gollum

Preheat the oven to 425 degrees. Place a 4 to 5 pound bluefish, cleaned and split, on an oiled baking sheet, skin side down. Lay 5 or 6 strips of bacon across it. Bake uncovered for 25 minutes until the fish flakes easily. Sprinkle with fresh parsley and lemon juice and serve immediately.

Seedcake for Gimli

Preheat the oven to 350 degrees. Butter an 8-inch round cake tin. Sift 2½ cups of flour with 1 teaspoon of baking powder and a pinch of salt. Cream together 4 ounces of butter and ¾ cup of sugar. Beat 1 egg and add to the butter, then add 2 teaspoons of caraway seeds. Fold in the flour mixture, then gradually add enough milk (up to ½ cup) to make a smooth, thick batter. Pour into the prepared pan. Bake in the middle of the oven for 45 minutes, or until a toothpick inserted in the center comes out clean. Let cool 5 to 10 minutes before turning out on a cake rack.

Goldberry's Pie

Heat the oven to 425 degrees. Mix ⅔ cup of sugar, 4 tablespoons of flour, ⅓ teaspoon of cinnamon, and a pinch of grated lemon peel. Mix with 3 cups of fresh berries (blueberries, blackberries, raspberries, strawberries, boysenberries). Pour into a pastry-lined pie

The Old Quick Post Service in Hobbiton

pan. Dot with butter. Cover with the top crust. Brush the top crust with milk and sprinkle with sugar. Bake for 35 to 45 minutes. If the crust begins to brown too much, cover the edges with tin foil.

Roast Mutton For The Trolls

Leave a thin layer of fat on a large leg of mutton and rub with a cut clove of garlic. Roast for 25 minutes per pound in a 350 degree oven. Serve with mint jelly and Shire pudding.

Shire Pudding

Mix together 1 cup of milk, 2 eggs, 1 cup of flour, and 1 teaspoon of salt in a blender. Put 3 tablespoons of hot beef or lamb drippings in a 9 inch glass pie plate. Pour the batter into the middle of the drippings. Bake in a preheated 425 degree oven for 15 minutes. Reduce the heat to 350 degrees and continue baking until the pudding is puffy and brown.

Tolkien of Affection

Two Puzzles

by Mel Rosen

ACROSS

1 Luzon volcano
5 Familiar initials in math
8 Hindu gentleman
12 —— on (urges)
16 Following
18 River to the Caspian
20 Zeal
21 Nov. 1957 space traveler
23 Who
27 Moroccan port
28 Word with welcome or place
29 Part of many German names
30 Fell for
31 Indian groom: Var.
32 Public warehouses
35 Usual food and drink
37 Three—— match
38 What
43 Westphalian city
44 Former French coin
45 Youngster
46 Canapé cover
49 Ruth's mother-in-law
52 Ingredient for 24 Down
56 When
63 Berne's river
64 Provokes sarcastically
65 Name in Dublin
66 Wax: comb. form
67 Gumshoes
68 Building extension
69 Caesar's greeting
70 Southeast Asian
71 Wages or reward, In N.Z.
72 English country festivals
74 Looking up
77 Worthless quantity of beans
78 Where
83 Old dirks
84 Competitor
85 Service ending
86 Air: Comb. form
88 Immobilize, in wrestling
89 Shock
93 Why
101 Watergate figure
102 Central point
103 Worshipful one
104 Cross
106 Tint
107 Word with up or off
108 Spinks's predecessor
109 A word considered only as letters or sounds
111 How
117 Luxury cut
118 Derby hopeful
119 New Haven draw
120 Kind of rocket
121 Coat-of-arms feature
122 Living-room item
123 A thing, in law
124 Org.

DOWN

1 William Howard and Robert A.
2 Nervous
3 "Right now!"
4 Sherpa perches
5 Books composed of sheets folded twice
6 Energy unit
7 Memorable U.N. name
8 Worst
9 Occurring by turns: Abbr.
10 Scrooge word
11 Rough
12 N.C. college
13 Salesman's gift
14 Asian ape
15 Enjoying the slopes
17 Louis Philippe, e.g.
19 Sweetened the soil
22 "——boy!"
24 Pilsener and lager
25 Boss Tweed's nemesis
26 Stopover
33 Certain vote
34 Medieval banner
35 Conclude
36 Chit
39 ——off (irate)
40 Half: Prefix
41 Comedienne Martha
42 Concept
46 Light carriage
47 Age tobacco
48 Very, to Pierre
50 Astern
51 Meditation syllables
53 File in a certain repository
54 Sneak home late
55 Excite
56 "Paper Moon" star and others
57 On —— (carousing)
58 Italian rooster
59 Swiss mathematician of the 1700's
60 Sap
61 Resided
62 Cold month in Madrid
70 Sci-fi movie of the 50's
73 Discord
74 Gun a motor
75 Wave, in Málaga
76 River of Argentina
79 Unhearing
80 Bone: Comb. form
81 Clue
82 What pride precedeth
87 "——La Mancha"
88 Pea package
90 72 for 18, usually
91 Glimpses of coming attractions: Var.
92 Tire city
93 Golden-rule words
94 Devonshire city
95 Subjects of conversation
96 Aura
97 Improve morally
98 Nagyvárad, to a Rumanian
99 Capek creations
100 Poetic sorrows
101 Letters from Greece
105 Exorcist's target
107 Lap dog, for short
108 Nick and Nora's dog
110 Lineman: Abbr.
112 "2001" feature
113 Milne creature
114 Sprite
115 Impair
116 Corrida cry

Solutions to puzzles on page 191.

DIRECTIONS:

An acrostic puzzle is not difficult to solve. If you can correctly guess as many as four or five WORDS, you have made a good start.

Each numbered blank represents one letter in the WORD to be defined. Answer as many WORDS as you can. Then copy the letters in each WORD to their corresponding numbered spaces in the diagram.

When completed, the diagram reads across only, showing a passage from a Tolkien book. The black squares indicate where a word ends and another begins. Words carry over to the next line if there is no black square at the end of a line.

You should discover words and phrases forming in the diagram as letters are filled in. Work backwards from the diagram to the WORDS, and in that way, guess still more WORDS. The letters in the upper right-hand corner of the squares in the diagram show the WORD from which a particular square's letter comes. The first letter of each WORD, in order, spells the complete name of the book from which the passage is taken.

1 B	2 N	■	3 X	4 J	5 L	■	6 C	7 B	8 N	9 H	10 Z	11 A	■	12 A	13 L	■
14 22	15 C	16 F	17 J	■	18 M	19 W	■	20 G	21 U	22 K	23 Q	24 Z	25 A	26 R	27 L	
28 L	29 P	30 V	31 G	32 Z	33 A	■	34 W	35 F	36 C	■	37 E	38 N	39 L	■	40 G	41 L
42 Y	■	43 O	44 E	45 F	46 R	47 N	■	48 I	49 X	50 B	51 S	■	52 N	53 E	54 Z	55 J
■	56 B	57 Y	■	58 A	59 W	60 Q	■	61 U	62 M	63 H	64 J	■	65 T	66 A	67 V	68 J
■	69 Y	70 G	■	71 M	72 Y	73 B	■	74 B	■	75 E	76 Z	77 I	78 P	79 J	80 T	
81 Z	82 C	83 U	84 K	■	85 Z	86 E	87 O	■	88 L	89 V	■	90 L	91 N	92 H	93 Z	94 E
■	95 I	96 T	97 W	98 V	99 C	■	100 K	101 A	102 Z	103 Q	104 O	■	105 Z	106 A	107 O	108 Q
109 L	110 F	111 Z	■	112 Q	113 Z2	■	114 U	115 L	116 K	■	117 V	118 M	119 X	120 D	■	121 N
122 V	123 F	■	124 O	125 F	126 W	127 R	■	128 J	129 V	■	130 G	130 S	132 Z	■	133 H	134 Z
135 S	136 F	■	137 Z	138 Q	139 I	■	140 J	141 N	142 Z	143 D	■	144 H	145 W	146 N	■	147 D
148 Q	149 Z	150 K	151 O	152 B	■	153 P	154 E	155 Z	156 H	■	157 V	158 I	■	159 I	160 X	161 L
162 E	163 W	164 C	165 Y	■	166 K	167 V	■	168 L	169 Z	170 N	171 J	■	172 F	173 Y	174 Q	175 N
176 P	■	177 Y	178 O	179 D	180 R	■	181 G	182 L	183 Q	184 U	185 Y	186 N	187 O	188 A	■	189 E
190 Z	191 J	192 L	■	193 V	194 D	195 P	■	196 C	197 P	198 Z	199 T	■	200 F	201 K	202 Z	
203 D	204 U	205 O	206 Z	207 F	■	208 D	■	209 A	210 U	211 L	212 D	213 Z	214 G	■	215 E	216 Z
217 S	■	218 N	219 H	■	220 E	221 Q	222 W	223 K	■	224 Z	225 J	226 A	■	227 C	228 X	

174

DEFINITIONS

WORDS

A. See Word Y.

— 33 — 58 — 66 — 101 — 11 — 12 — 226 — 106 — 209 — 188 — 25

B. Commemorative occasion

— 1 — 7 — 50 — 56 — 73 — 74 — 152

C. Town on Long Lake, below the Lonely Mountain

— 164 — 196 — 6 — 15 — 36 — 82 — 99 — 227

D. Came to pass

— 194 — 208 — 212 — 143 — 120 — 203 — 179 — 147

E. Insulting name for a spider (2 words)

— 189 — 75 — 215 — 37 — 154 — 220 — 86 — 44 — 162 — 94 — 53

F. Old Took's great-granduncle

— 200 — 45 — 172 — 110 — 123 — 35 — 125 — 207 — 136 — 16

G. Moistened

— 40 — 31 — 181 — 214 — 130 — 70 — 20

H. Feasting and total comfort, to Bilbo Baggins

— 63 — 156 — 219 — 144 — 9

I. Added a spigot, to a cider barrel perhaps

— 77 — 95 — 159 — 48 — 158 — 139

J. Thorin's last name

— 225 — 4 — 17 — 191 — 64 — 55 — 171 — 128 — 68 — 79 — 140

K. Paid back; took vengeance

— 22 — 116 — 100 — 201 — 166 — 84 — 223 — 150

L. "——, the spear is long, the arrow swift, the Gate is strong" (4 words from a song of the dwarves)

— 109 — 115 — 28 — 27 — 168 — 39 — 90 — 161

— 41 — 5 — 13 — 88 — 182 — 192 — 211

M. Sound of laughter

— 71 — 18 — 92 — 62 — 118 — 133

N. Line of demarcation near the Misty Mountains (4 words)

| 2 | 47 | 175 | 52 | 91 | 121 | 170 | 218 | 141 | 38 | 186 | 8 | 146 |

O. Elrond's Last Homely House

| 43 | 107 | 205 | 178 | 187 | 87 | 104 | 151 | 124 |

P. Stimulate

| 176 | 29 | 153 | 197 | 78 | 195 |

Q. The Heart of the Mountain, buried with Thorin

| 221 | 174 | 23 | 108 | 183 | 60 | 103 | 112 | 138 | 148 |

R. The Shire, to Bilbo; The Lonely Mountain, to Smaug

| 46 | 127 | 26 | 180 |

S. Smaug, after the black arrow

| 135 | 51 | 131 | 217 |

T. Complain

| 96 | 199 | 80 | 65 |

U. Stir up

| 83 | 184 | 210 | 61 | 21 | 114 | 204 |

V. "——and tread on the fat! Pour the milk on the pantry floor!" (3 words from another song)

| 30 | 98 | 129 | 193 | 69 | 89 | 67 | 117 | 122 | 167 | 157 |

W. "Elves and Men! To me! O my——" (rallying cry during the Battle of Five Armies)

| 222 | 59 | 145 | 19 | 34 | 97 | 163 | 126 |

X. Watchful; observant

| 160 | 3 | 49 | 119 | 228 |

Y. The wandering wizard

| 42 | 72 | 57 | 165 | 173 | 185 | 177 |

Z. Relative of water skis

| 137 | 105 | 10 | 85 | 32 | 213 | 149 | 224 | 54 |

Z1. Quality imparted by a ring

| 102 | 24 | 190 | 216 | 132 | 134 | 81 | 76 | 155 | 169 | 202 | 111 |

Z2. In demand; craved

| 113 | 93 | 142 | 14 | 206 | 198 |

Solutions to puzzles on page 191.

Appendix

A Gathering of Fans

Listed below are some of the major national and international Tolkien and fantasy societies, as well as two of the more long-lived university groups. For further information on regional science fiction and fantasy clubs, the best source is a directory compiled by the Los Angeles Science Fantasy Society. The society welcomes inquiries and new listings, which should be directed to: The Los Angeles Science Fantasy Society, 11513 Burbank Boulevard, North Hollywood, California 91601.

The American Tolkien Society
1408 Caprice, Union Lake, Michigan 48085. Publishes *Appendix* (monthly) and *Minas Tirith Evening-Star* (quarterly). Dues are $5 per year.

The Mythopoeic Society
P.O. Box 4671, Whittier, California 90607. Publishes a monthly newsletter, *Mythprint,* and *Mythlore,* a scholarly journal. Dues are $8 per year.

The National Fantasy Fan Federation
Mrs. Jane Lamb, Route #1, Box 364, Heiskell, Tennessee 37754. Publishes *The National Fantasy Fan* (monthly) and *Tightbeam* (bimonthly), as well as a collectors' bulletin. Dues are $3 per year.

The University of Wisconsin Tolkien Society
c/o Jeffrey Painter, 723 Pitman, Witte Hall, Madison, Wisconsin 53706. Member Richard West publishes *Orcrist.*

The British Fantasy Society
Brian Mooney, 447A Porters Avenue, Dagenham, Essex RM9 4ND, United Kingdom. Publishes *Dark Horizons* (monthly).

The Tolkien Society
14 Norfolk Avenue, London N15 6JX, England. Publishes *Amon Hen* (bimonthly) and *Mallorn* (annual).

The Sydney University Tolkien Society
Box 272, Wentworth Building, University of Sydney, New South Wales 2006, Australia. Publishes *The Eye.*

A Fan's Reading List

The publications issued to members of the various Tolkien societies are a good introduction to the small magazines and newsletters that go by the name of fanzines. As you'll see from the brief list below, fanzines are alive and flourishing. For a more complete listing of these publications, consult *The Little Gem Guide to Fanzines,* available from Peter Roberts, 38 Oakland Drive, Dawlish, Devon, United Kingdom.

Checkpoint
Edited and produced by Peter Roberts, 38 Oakland Drive, Dawlish, Devon, England. Monthly. $1 for 5 issues.

Delap's F and SF Review
Edited by Richard Delap, 11863 West Jefferson Boulevard, Culver City, California 90230. Monthly. $9 per year (individuals); $12 per year (institutions).

Extrapolation: A Journal of Science Fiction and Fantasy
Edited by Thomas D. Clareson, Box 3186, The College of Wooster, Wooster, Ohio 44691. Biannual. $4 for 2 issues.

Fan's Zine
Edited by Wally Stoelting, 2326 Deewood Drive, Columbus, Ohio 43229. Monthly. $.30 apiece.

Fantasy Newsletter
Published by Paul Allen, 1015 West 36th Street, Loveland, Colorado 80537. Monthly. $5 per year.

Fanzine Fanatique
Published by Keith and Rosemary Walker, 2 Daisy Bank, Quernmore Road, Lancaster, Lancashire, England. Bimonthly.

File 770
Published by Mike Glyer, 14974 Osceola Street, Sylmar, California 91342. $1.50 for 4 issues.

Forthcoming SF Books
Published by Joanne Burger, 55 Blue Bonnet Court, Lake Jackson, Texas 77566. Published bimonthly. $2 per year.

Foundation: The Review of Science Fiction
Edited by Peter Nicholls, The Science Fiction Foundation, North East London Polytechnic, Longbridge Road, Essex RM8 2AS, England. Triannual.

Locus
Edited and published by Charles and Dena Brown, P. O. Box 3938, San Francisco, California 94119. Appears fifteen times a year. $9 per year.

Luna
Edited by Ann F. Dietz, 655 Orchard Street, Oradell, New Jersey 07649. Quarterly. $3 per year.

Niekas
Published by Ed Meskys, R. F. #1, Box 3, Center Harbor, New Hampshire 03226.

Noumenon
Edited and published by Brian Thurogood, Wilma Road, Ostend, Waiheke Island, Hauraki Gulf, New Zealand. Monthly. $10.75 for 10 issues (air mail); $5.50 for 10 issues (sea mail).

Outworlds
Edited and published by Bill Bowers, P.O. Box 2521, North Canton, Ohio 44720. Quarterly. $5 for 4 issues.

Riverside Quarterly
Edited by Leland Sapiro, Box 14451, University Station, Gainesville, Florida 32604. Irregular. $2 for 4 copies.

Rune
Published by the Minnesota Science Fiction Society. Edited by David Emerson, 343 East 19th Street, #1B, Minneapolis, Minnesota 55404. Quarterly. $.50 per copy.

Science Fiction Review
Edited and published by Richard Geis, P. O. Box 11408, Portland, Oregon 97211. Quarterly. $4.50 for 4 issues.

Science Fiction Studies
Edited by R.D. Mullen and Darko Suvin, English Department, Indiana State University, Terre Haute, Indiana 47809. Triannual. $7 per year.

The Spang Blah
Published by Jan Howard Finder, P.O. Box 428, Latham, New York 12110. Quarterly. $.75 per issue; $3 for 5 issues.

Wyrd: The Magazine of Illustrated Fantasy
Published by Greg Stafford, P.O. Box 6302, Albany, California 94706. Irregular. $6 for 3 issues.

Yandro
Published by Robert and Juanita Coulson, Route 3, Hartford City, Indiana 47348. Irregular. $3 for 5 issues.

A Tolkien Bibliography

by

Bonniejean Christensen

Tolkien's Scholarly Works

"Ancrene Wisse and Hali Meidhed," *Essays and Studies of the English Association,* O. S. XIV (1929), 104–126.

Ancrene Wisse: The English Text of the Ancrene Riwle, edited from MA Corpus Christi College, Cambridge 402, with an introduction by N. R. Ker. London: Oxford University Press, 1962. (Early English Text Society, Original Series No. 249.)

"*Beowulf:* The Monsters and the Critics," *Proceedings of the British Academy,* XXII (1936), 245–295. Reprinted in *An Anthology of Beowulf Criticism,* ed. Lewis E. Nicholson, Notre Dame: University of Notre Dame Press, 1963, and *The Beowulf Poet: A Collection of Critical Essays,* ed. Donald K. Fry, Englewood Cliffs, N.J.: Prentice-Hall, Inc., 1968.

"Chaucer as Philologist: *The Reeve's Tale,*" *Transactions of the Philological Society,* 1934, pp. 1–70.

"The Devil's Coach-Horses" (notes on Middle English *aeveres*), *Review of English Studies,* 1 (July 1925), 331–336.

"English and Welsh," introductory lecture of *Angles and Britons,* pp. 1–41, The O'Donnell Lectures, Vol. 1. Cardiff: University of Wales Press, 1963; Mystic, Conn.: Verry, Lawrence, Inc., 1963.

"Fantasy" (a selection from the revised essay "On Fairy-Stories), pp. 202–207, in *Pastoral and Romance: Modern Essays in Criticism,* ed. by Eleanor Terry Lincoln. New York: Prentice-Hall, 1969.

"For W.H.A." *Shenandoah,* XVIII (Winter 1967), 96–97.

"Foreword" to *A New Glossary of the Dialect of the Huddersfield District* by Walter E. Haigh. Oxford: University Press, 1928.

"Henry Bradley, 3 December, 1845–23 May, 1923" (obituary), *Bulletin of the Modern Humanities Research Association,* No. 20 (October 1923), pp. 4–5.

"The Homecoming of Beorhtnoth Beorhthelm's Son," *Essays and Studies of the English Association,* N. S. VI (1953), 1–18. Reprinted in *The Tolkien Reader.*

"The Lay of Aotrou and Itoun," *Welsh Review,* IV (December 1945), 254–266.

"Middle English 'Losenger': Sketch of an Etymological and Semantic Enquiry," *Essais de Philologie Moderne* (Paris: Société d'edition "Les Belles Lettres," 1953), pp. 63–76.

A Middle English Vocabulary. London: Milford, 1920; Oxford: Clarendon Press, 1922; Oxford: University Press, 1956. Prepared for use with *Fourteenth Century Verse and Prose,* ed. Kenneth Sisam (Oxford: Clarendon Press, 1921) and included in later editions as the Glossary.

"On Fairy-Stories," in *Essays Presented to Charles Williams,* pp. 38–89, ed. C.S. Lewis, London: Oxford University Press, 1947; Grand Rapids, Michigan: William B. Eardmans Publishing Co., 1966. Revised for *Tree and Leaf* and reprinted in *The Tolkien Reader.*

"Preface" to *The Ancrene Riwle,* translated into Modern English by M.B. Salu, with an introduction by Dom Gerard Sitwell, O.S.B. Notre Dame: University of Notre Dame Press, 1956.

"Prefatory Remarks" to *Beowulf and the Finnesburg Fragment, A Translation into Modern English Prose,* by John R. Clark Hall. London: G. Allen and Unwin, 1940; 1950.

"Sigelwara Land: Part I," *Medium Aevum,* I (December 1932), 183–196.

"Sigelwara Land: Part II," *Medium Aevum,* III (June 1934), 95–111.

Sir Gawain and the Green Knight, ed. with E.V. Gordon. Oxford: Clarendon Press, 1925. 2nd ed. revised by Norman Davis. London: Oxford University Press, 1967.

Sir Gawain and the Green Knight; Pearl; and Sir Orfeo. Boston: Houghton Mifflin, 1975.

"Some Contributions to Middle-English Lexicography," *Review of English Studies,* I (April 1925), 210–15.

Songs for the Philologists, by E. V. Gordon *et al.,* privately printed by the Department of English at University College, London, 1936.

Tolkien's Popular Works

The Adventures of Tom Bombadil and Other Verses from the Red Book, illus. by Pauline Baynes. London: G. Allen and Unwin, 1962; Toronto: Thomas Nelson and Sons, 1962; Boston: Houghton Mifflin, 1963. Reprinted in *The Tolkien Reader.*

"Bilbo's Song," a poem from *The Return of the King,* reprinted in *Practical English,* XLII (March 17, 1967), 8.

"The Dragon's Visit" (poem), pp. 257–262 in *The Young Magicians,* ed. by Lin Carter. New York: Ballantine, 1969.

Farmer Giles of Ham, illus. by Pauline Baynes. London: G. Allen and Unwin, 1949; Boston: Houghton Mifflin, 1950. Reprinted in *The Tolkien Reader* and in *Smith of Wootton Major and Farmer Giles of Ham.*

The Fellowship of the Ring; Being the First Part of The Lord of the Rings. See *The Lord of the Rings.*

The Hobbit; or, There and Back Again, illus. by the author. London: G. Allen and Unwin, 1937; 1951; Boston: Houghton Mifflin, 1938, 1958; New York: Ballantine Books, 1965, 1966; London: Longmans Green, 1966.

"Imram" (verse dialogue between St. Brendan and inquirer), illus. by Robert Gibbings, *Time and Tide,* XXXVI (December 3, 1955), 1561.

"Leaf by Niggle," *Dublin Review,* CCXVI (January 1945), 26–61. Reprinted in *Tree and Leaf* and *The Tolkien Reader.*

"A Letter from J.R.R. Tolkien," pp. 221–222 in The Image of Man in C.S. Lewis by William Luther White. Nashville, Tennessee: Abingdon Press, 1969.

The Lord of the Rings. 3 vols. London: G. Allen and Unwin, 1954–55; Toronto: Thomas Nelson and Sons, 1954–55; Boston: Houghton Mifflin, 1954–56; New York: Ace Books, 1965. *Ibid.* Rev. ed. New York: Ballantine Books, 1965. *Ibid.* 2nd ed. London: G. Allen and Unwin, 1966; Boston: Houghton Mifflin, 1967. *Ibid.* 1 vol. paperback, omitting the Appendices except for "Aragorn and Arwen." London: G. Allen and Unwin, 1968.

"Once Upon a Time" (poem), pp. 254–256 in *The Young Magicians,* ed. Lin Carter. New York: Ballantine, 1969.

The Return of the King; Being the Third Part of The Lord of the Rings. See *The Lord of the Rings.*

"Riddles in the Dark," Chapter V of the first edition of The Hobbit, reprinted in *Just for Fun: Humorous Stories and Poems,* ed. Elva S. Smith and Alice I. Hazeltin, New York: Lothrop, Lee and Shepard, 1948, and *Anthology of Children's Literature,* ed. Edna Johnson, Evelyn R. Sickles, and Frances Clarke Sayer, Boston: Houghton Mifflin, 1959.

The Road Goes Ever On: A Song Cycle, with poems by Tolkien and music by Donald Swann. London: G. Allen and Unwin, 1967; Boston: Houghton Mifflin, 1967.

The Silmarillion. London: G. Allen and Unwin, 1977; Boston: Houghton Mifflin, 1977.

Smith of Wootton Major, illus. by Pauline Baynes. London: G. Allen and Unwin, 1967; Boston: Houghton Mifflin, 1967. *Ibid.,* illus. by Milton Glaser, *Redbook,* CXXX (December 1967), 58–61, 101, 103–107.

Smith of Wooton Major and Farmer Giles of Ham, illus. by Pauline Baines. New York: Ballantine Books, 1969.

"Tolkien on Tolkien," *Diplomat,* XVIII (October 1966), 39.

The Tolkien Reader, with an introduction, "Tolkien's Magic Ring," by Peter S. Beagle, and reprints of "The Homecoming of Beorhtnoth Beorhthelm's Son," *Farmer Giles of Ham, The Adventures of Tom Bombadil,* and *Tree and Leaf.* New York: Ballantine Books, 1966.

Tree and Leaf, containing "Leaf by Niggle" and a revised "On Fairy-Stories." London: G. Allen and Unwin, 1964; Boston: Houghton Mifflin, 1965. Reprinted in *The Tolkien Reader.*

The Two Towers: Being the Second Part of The Lord of the Rings. See *The Lord of the Rings.*

Colby, Vineta. "J.R.R. Tolkien" (biographical sketch), *Wilson Library Bulletin,* XXXI (June 1957), 768.

Auden, W.H. "Making and Judging Poetry," *Atlantic Monthly,* CXCIX (January 1957) 44–52.

Beard, Henry N. and Douglas C. Kenney. *Bored of the Rings: A Parody of J.R.R. Tolkien's The Lord of the Rings [The Harvard Lampoon].* New York: Signet Books, 1969; New York: New American Library, 1971.

Beatie, Bruce A. "The Tolkien Phenomenon," *Niekas,* October 1967, pp. 4–5, 8.

Carter, Lin. *J.R.R. Tolkien: A Look Behind "The Lord of the Rings".* New York: Ballantine Books, 1969.

———. *Middle Earth: The World of Tolkien.* Illus. New York: Centaur, 1977.

Castell, Daphne. "The Realms of Tolkien," *New Worlds,* L (November 1966), 143–154.

Crist, Judith Klein. "Why 'Frodo Lives'," *Ladies Home Journal, LXXXIV (February 1967), 58.*

Cullen, Tom A. "Live in 'Middle Earth': British Hobbits Become Idols of American Youth," (Madison, Wisconsin) *Capital Times,* Friday, April 26, 1968, Green Sheet, 1.

Del Ray, Lester. "A Report on J.R.R. Tolkien," *Worlds of Fantasy,* I (October 1968), 84–85.

Duff, Annis. *Longer Flight: A Family Grows Up with Books.* New York: Viking Press, 1955.

Eaton, Anne Thaxter. *Reading with Children* (biographical note, pp. 19–23). New York: Viking Press, 1940.

Elliott, Charles. "Can America Kick the Hobbit?: The Tolkien Caper," *Life,* LXII (February 24, 1967), 10.

Ellman, Mary. "Growing Up Hobbitic," *New American Review* No. 2 (New American Library, 1968), pp. 217–229.

"The Elvish Mode." *New Yorker,* XLI (January 15, 1966), 24–25.

Evans, W.D. Emrys. "The Lord of the Rings," *The School Librarian,* XVI (December 1968), 284–288.

Fuller, Muriel, ed. "J.R.R. Tolkien," *More Junior Authors.* New York: Wilson, 1963.

Glixon, David M. "Your Literary I.Q." (word game) featuring "Frodo Lives," submitted by Susan Reisner, *Saturday Reivew,* LII (January 3, 1970), 78–83.

Gray, Patricia Clark. *J.R.R. Tolkien's The Hobbit* (dramatization). Chicago: Dramatic Publishing Co., 1968.

Griffin, Nancy. "The Fellowship of Hobbitomanes," *San Francisco Sunday Examiner and Chronicle,* "This World" section, pp. 44, 51, and cover.

Grigson, Geoffrey, ed. "J.R.R. Tolkien," *The Concise Encyclopedia of Modern World Literature.* New York: Hawthorn Books, 1963.

Haas, Joseph. "Exploring the Heart of Tolkien's Allegory" (rev. of *The Tolkien Relation*), *Chicago Daily News,* May 4, 1968, p. 9.

Harshaw, Ruth. "When Carnival of Books Went to Europe," *ALA Bulletin,* LI (February 1957), 117–123.

Henniker-Heaton, Peter J. "Tolkien Disguised as Himself" (rev. of *The Tolkien Relation*), *Christian Science Monitor,* Thursday, May 23, 1968, p. 7.

"The Hobbit Habit." *Time,* LXXXCIII (July 15, 1966), 48, 51.

Huber, Miriam Blanton. *Story and Verse for Children.* 3rd ed. New York: Macmillan, 1966.

Johnson, Edna, Evelyn R. Sickels, and Frances Clarke Sayer, eds. "J.R.R. Tolkien," in *Anthology of Children's Literature.* 3rd ed. Boston: Houghton Mifflin, 1959.

"J.R.R. Tolkien." *Britannica Book of the Year,* 1967, p. 167.

"J.R.R. Tolkien." *Contemporary Authors,* XVII-XVIII, 394-396.

"J.R.R. Tolkien." *Current Biography Yearbook,* XVIII (1957), 555-556.

"J.R.R. Tolkien." *Current Biography Yearbook,* XXVIII (1967), 415-418.

"J.R.R. Tolkien." *Guide To Catholic Literature, 1880-1940,* p. 1141.

"John R. Tunis and John R.R. Tolkien," *New York Herald Tribune Books,* May 1, 1938, p. 8.

Lauritsen, Frederick Michael. Rev. of *The Tolkien Relation, Library Journal,* XCIII (May, 1968), 1889.

Lewis, C.S. *Surprised by Joy; the Shape of My Early Life.* New York: Harcourt, Brace, 1956.

"Marquette Library Has Papers of Tolkien, Hobbits' Creator." *The Marquette Tribune,* LII (Friday, December 15, 1967), 3. (Interview-article with Fr. Raphael N. Hamilton, S.J., archivist.)

Mathewson, Joseph. "The Hobbit Habit," illus. by David Levine, *Esquire,* LXVI (September 1966), 130-131, 221-222.

Menen, Aubrey. "Learning to Love the Hobbits," *Diplomat,* XVIII (October 1966), 32-34, 37-38.

Millin, Leslie. "Who in the Name of Orcs and Hobbits is Tolkien?" (Toronto) *Globe Magazine,* March 2, 1968, pp. 4-7.

Morrison, Louis. *Monarch Literature Notes on Tolkien's Fellowship of the Ring* New York: Monarch Press, 1976.

Norman, Philip. "The Hobbitman," *London Sunday Times Magazine,* January 15, 1967, pp. 34-36. Reprinted as "The Prevalence of Hobbits," *New York Times Magazine,* Sunday, January 15, 1967, pp. 30-31, 97, 100, 102.

Piggin, Julia R. "Desirers of Dragons," illus. by Tom Eaton, *Practical English,* XLII (March 17, 1967), 4-7.

Plotz, Richard Douglas. "Face to Face: With R.D. Plotz, Founder of Tolkien Society of America," *Seventeen,* XXV (April 1966), 153.

"Professor Tolkien and the Hobbits." *Diplomat,* XVIII (October 1966), 31-43, 73-74.

Ready, William. "The Tolkien Relation," *Canadian Library,* XXV (September 1968), 128-136.

———. *The Tolkien Relation: A Personal Inquiry.* Chicago: Henry Regnery, 1968. Reissued as *Understanding Tolkien and The Lord of the Rings.* New York: Paperback Library, 1969.

—. *Understanding Tolkien and The Lord of the Rings.* New York: Warner Books, 1976.

Resnik, Henry. "The Hobbit-Forming World of J.R.R. Tolkien," *Saturday Evening Post,* CCXXXIX (July 2, 1966), 90–94.

Schmidt, Sandra. "Taking Fairy Tales Seriously," *Christian Science Monitor,* LVI (April 15, 1965), 7.

Smith, Nancy. "The Pleasures of the Hobbit Table," *Diplomat,* XVIII (October 1966), 42–43, 73–74.

Stein, Ruth M. "The Changing Styles in Dragons—From Fafnir to Smaug," *Elementary English,* XLV (February 1968), 179–183, 189.

Stewart, Douglas J. "The Hobbit War," *Nation,* (October 9, 1967), 332–334.

Strothman, Janet. Rev. of *The Tolkien Relation. Library Journal,* XCIII (July 1968), 2743.

"Tolkien's Mythology Comes to Vietnam," *Publisher's Weekly,* CXCII (September 4, 1967), 24.

Torrens, James. "With Tolkien in Middle-earth," *Good Work,* XXXI (Winter 1968), 17–23.

"Wacky World of Tolkien Catching On With Youth." (Los Angeles) *Times,* Wednesday, August 31, 1966, Part V, p. 4.

Waggoner, Diana. *The Hills of Faraway: A Guide to Fantasy.* New York: Atheneum, 1978.

Wain, John. *Sprightly Running.* London: Macmillan, 1963.

Wojcik, Jan. 'Tolkien's Lord-of-Rings Quest Likened to Christmas Gospel," (Boston) *Pilot,* December 24, 1966, p. 8.

Scholarly Works on Tolkien's Fiction

Auden, W.H. "Good and Evil in *The Lord of the Rings,*" *Tolkien Journal,* III (Spring 1967), 5–8. Reprinted in *Critical Quarterly,* X (1968), 138–142.

—. "The Quest Hero," *Texas Quarterly,* IV (Winter 1961), 81–93. Reprinted in Isaacs and Zimbardo, pp. 40–61

Barber, Dorothy Elizabeth Klein. "The Meaning of *The Lord of the Rings,*" *Mankato State College Studies,* II (February 1967), 38–50.

—. "The Structure of *The Lord of the Rings.*" Unpublished doctoral dissertation. University of Michigan, 1966.

Beatie, Bruce A. "Folk Tale, Fiction, and Saga in J.R.R. Tolkien's *The Lord of the Rings,*" *Mankato State College Studies,* II (February 1967), 1–17.

—. "J.R.R. Tolkien's *Lord of the Rings* and the Traditional Epic," a paper read at the Rocky Mountain Modern Language Association at the University of Utah, October 14–15, 1966.

—. *"The Lord of the Rings:* Myth, Reality, and Relevance," *Western Review,* IV (Winter 1967), 58–59.

Bisenieks, Dainis, "Reading and Misreading Tolkien," *Mankato State College Studies,* II (February 1967), 98–100.

Blackmun, Kathryn. "The Development of Runic and Feanorian

Alphabets for the Transliteration of English," *Mankato State College Studies,* II (February 1967), 76–83.

———. "Translations from the Elvish" (a lexicon and translation for "A Elberth Gilthoniel"), *Mankato State College Studies,* II (February 1967), 95–97.

Blissett, William Frank. "Despots of the Rings," *South Atlantic Quarterly,* LVIII (Summer 1959), 448–456.

Bradley, Marion Zimmer. "Men, Halflings, and Hero Worship," *Niekas* #16 (June 1966), pp. 25–44. Revised essay appears in Isaacs and Zimbardo, 109–127.

Briggs, K.M. *The Fairies in English Tradition and Literature.* Chicago: University of Chicago Press. 1967.

Carpenter, Humphrey. *Tolkien: A Biography.* London: George Allen and Unwin, 1977; Boston: Houghton Mifflin, 1977.

Christensen, Bonniejean. "An Ace Mystery: Did Tolkien Write His Own Retraction?" *Orcrist,* 4 (1970), 16.

———. "Adventures in Manipulation," *English Journal,* 60 (March 1971), 359–360.

———. *Beowulf and The Hobbit: Elegy into Fantasy in J.R.R. Tolkien's Creative Technique.* Unpublished doctoral dissertation. University of Southern California, 1969.

———. "Gollum's Character Transformation in *The Hobbit,*" in *A Tolkien Compass,* ed. Jared Lobdell. La Salle, Ill.: Open Court Publishing Co., 1975.

———. "Gracia Fay Ellwood's *Good News from Tolkien's Middle Earth,*" *Christian Scholar's Review,* 1 (Spring 1971), 285–286.

———. "J.R.R. Tolkien: A Bibliography," *Bulletin of Bibliography,* 27 (July-September 1970), 61–67.

———. "A Ready Answer," *Tolkien Journal*, 10 (November 1969), 15–17.

———. "Report from the West: Exploitation of *The Hobbit,*" *Orcrist,* 4 (1970), 15–16.

———. "Tolkien's Creative Technique: *Beowulf* and *The Hobbit,*" *Orcrist,* 7 (1972), 16–20.

Crouch, Marcus S. *Treasure Seekers and Borrowers: Children's Books in Britain, 1900–1960.* London: Library Association, 1962.

Ellwood, Gracia Fay, *Good News from Tolkien's Middle Earth.* Grand Rapids, Michigan: William B. Eerdmans Publishing Co., 1970.

Evans, Robley. *J.R.R. Tolkien.* New York: Warner Paperback Library, 1972; New York: Thomas Y. Crowell, 1976.

Everett, Caroline Whitman. "The Imaginative Fiction of J.R.R. Tolkien." Unpublished master's thesis. Florida State University, 1957.

Eyre, Frank. *Twentieth Century Children's Books.* London and New York: Longmans, Green, 1952.

Fisher, Margery. *Intent Upon Reading: A Critical Appraisal of Modern Fiction for Children.* Leicester: Brockhampton, 1961; New York: F. Watts, 1962.

Foster, Robert A. *A Guide to Middle Earth.* Ballantine, 1975. Originally published as *A Guide to Middle-Earth: A Glossary and Concordance of the Works of J.R.R. Tolkien.* New York: Mirage Press, 1971.

Fuller, Edmund. "The Lord of the Hobbits: J.R.R. Tolkien," in his *Books with Men Behind Them,* pp. 169–196. New York: Random House, 1959. Slightly revised essay appears in Isaacs and Zimbardo, pp. 17–39.

Garmon, Gerald. "J.R.R. Tolkien's Modern Fairyland," *West Georgia College Review,* IV (May 1973).

Gasque, Thomas J. "Tolkien: The Monsters and the Critters," pp. 151–163 in Isaacs and Zimbardo.

Geijerstam, Carl-Erik af. "Anteckningar om J.R.R. Tolkien's saga-epos Ringen," *Studiekamraten,* XLIX (1967), 90.

Green, Roger Lancelyn. "Reluctant Dragons" in his *Authors and Places: A Literary Pilgrimage.* New York: G.P. Putnam's Sons, 1963.

———. *Tellers of Tales: Children's Books and Their Authors from 1800 to 1964.* Rev. ed. London: Edmund Ward, 1965.

Grotta, Daniel. *J.R.R. Tolkien: Architect of Middle Earth.* Philadelphia: Running Press, 1976 (revised edition, 1978); New York: Warner Books, 1977.

Hayes, Noreen, and Robert Renshaw. "Of Hobbits: *The Lord of the Rings,*" *Critique: Studies in Modern Fiction,* IX (1967), 58–66.

Hedges, Ned Samuel. "The Fable and the Fabulous: The Use of Traditional Forms in Children's Literature." Unpublished doctoral dissertation. University of Nebraska at Lincoln, 1968.

Helms, Randel. *Tolkien's World.* Boston: Houghton Mifflin, 1974.

Irwin, William Robert. "There and Back Again: The Romances of Williams, Lewis, and Tolkien," *Sewanee Review,* LXIX (Fall 1961), 566–578.

Isaacs, Neil D. "On the Possibilities of Writing Tolkien Criticism," pp. 1–11 in Isaacs and Zimbardo.

Isaacs, Neil D., and Rose A. Zimbardo, eds. *Tolkien and the Critics.* Notre Dame, Indiana: University of Notre Dame Press, 1968.

Johnston, George Burke. "The Poetry of J.R.R. Tolkien," *Mankato State College Studies,* II (February 1967), 63–73.

Keenan, Hugh T. "The Appeal of *The Lord of the Rings:* A Struggle for Life," pp. 62–80 in Isaacs and Zimbardo.

Kelly, Mary Quella. "The Poetry of Fantasy: Verse in *The Lord of the Rings,*" pp. 170–200 in Isaacs and Zimbardo.

Kilby, Clyde S. *Tolkien and the Silmarillion.* Wheaton, Ill.: Shaw Publishers, 1976.

———. "Tolkien as Scholar and Artist," *Tolkien Journal,* III (Spring 1967), 9–11.

Kocher, Paul Harold. *Master of Middle-earth: The Fiction of J.R.R. Tolkien.* Boston: Houghton Mifflin, 1972.

Léaud, Francis. "L'Épopée Religieuse de J.R.R. Tolkien," *Etudes Anglaises,* XXX (1967), 267–281.

Levitin, Alexis. "The Hero in J.R.R. Tolkien's *The Lord of the*

Rings," *Mankato State College Studies,* II (February 1967), 25–37.

———. "The Lord of the Rings." Unpublished master's thesis. Columbia University, 1964.

Lewis, W.H., ed. *Letters of C.S. Lewis.* London: Geoffrey Bles, 1966; New York: Harcourt, Brace and World, 1966.

Lobdell, Jared C. "From Middle-Earth to the Silent Planet," [Milwaukee] *Rally,* II (July-August 1967), 36–37.

———. "Good and Evil for Men and Hobbits" (rev. of Isaacs and Lombardo), *National Review,* XXI (June 17, 1969), 605.

———. "J.R.R. Tolkien: Words That Sound Like Castles," [Milwaukee] *Rally* I (August 1966), 24–26.

———., ed. *A Tolkien Compass.* La Salle, Ill.: Open Court Publishing Co., 1975.

Lupoff, Richard A. *Edgar Rice Burroughs: Master of Adventure* (quotations from Tolkien's response to Lupoff). New York: Canaveral Press, 1965; New York: Ace, 1968.

Melmed, Susan Barbara. *J.R.R. Tolkien; A Bibliography.* Johannesburg: University of the Witwatersrand, 1972.

Miesel, Sandra L. "Some Motifs and Sources for *Lord of the Rings,"* *Riverside Quarterly,* III (March 1968), 125–128.

———. "Some Religious Aspects of *Lord of the Rings,"* *Riverside Quarterly,* III (August 1968), 209–213.

Miller, David M. "The Moral Universe of J.R.R. Tolkien," *Mankato State College Studies*, II (February 1967), 51–62.

Moorman, Charles. *The Book of Kyng Arthur: The Unity of Malory's Morte Darthur* (anecdote about Tolkien's revisions, p. xxix). Lexington, Kentucky: University of Kentucky Press, 1965.

———. "The Shire, Mordor, and Minas Tirith: J.R.R. Tolkien," pp. 86–100 in his *The Precincts of Felicity: The Augustinian City of the Oxford Christians.* Gainesville: University of Florida Press, 1966. Reprinted in Isaacs and Zimbardo, pp. 201–217.

Norwood, W.D. "Tolkien's Intention in *The Lord of the Rings*," *Mankato State College Studies,* II (February 1967), 18–24.

Ottevaere-van Praag, Ganna. "Retour a l'épopée mythologique: *Le Maitre des Anneaux de* J.R.R. Tolkien," *Revue des Langues Vivantes* [Bruxelles], XXXIII (1967), 237–245.

Raffel, Burton. *"The Lord of the Rings* as Literature," pp. 218–246 in Isaacs and Zimbardo.

Rang, Jack C. "Two Servants," *Mankato State College Studies,* II (February 1967), 84–94.

Reilly, Robert J. "Romantic Religion in the Works of Owen Barfield, C.S. Lewis, Charles Williams, and J.R.R. Tolkien," Unpublished doctoral dissertation. Michigan State University, 1960.

———. "Tolkien and the Fairy Story," *Thought,* XXXVIII (Spring 1963), 89–106. Reprinted in Isaacs and Zimbardo, pp. 128–150.

Reinken, Donald L. "J.R.R. Tolkien's *The Lord of the Rings:* A Christian Refounding of the Political Order," *Christian Perspectives: An Ecumenical Quarterly,* Winter 1966, pp. 16–23.

Roberts, Mark. "Adventure in English" (on *The Lord of the Rings), Essays in Criticism,* VI (October 1956), 450–459.

Russell, Mariann Barbara. "The Idea of the City of God." Unpublished doctoral dissertation. Columbia University, 1965.

Ryan, J.S. "German Mythology Applied—The Extension of the Literary Folk Memory," *Folklore,* LXXVII (Spring 1966), 45–59.

Sale, Roger, "England's Parnassus: C.S. Lewis, Charles Williams, and J.R.R. Tolkien," *Hudson Review,* XVII (Summer 1964), 203–225.

———. *Modern Heroism: Essays on D.H. Lawrence, William Empson, and J.R.R. Tolkien.* Berkeley: University of California Press, 1973.

———. "Tolkien and Frodo Baggins," pp. 247–288 in Isaacs and

Zimbardo.

Scott, Nathan A., Jr. "Poetry and Prayer," *Thought,* XLI (Spring 1966), 61–80.

Spacks, Patricia Meyer. "Ethical Pattern in *The Lord of the Rings.*" *Critique: Studies in Modern Fiction,* III (Spring-Fall 1959), 30–42. Revised and reprinted as "Power and Meaning in *The Lord of the Rings,*" Isaacs and Zimbardo, pp. 81–99.

Stein, Ruth M. Letter to the editor in reply to W.L. Taylor, *English Journal,* LVII (February 1968), 818–821.

Stimpson, Catharine R. *J.R.R. Tolkien.* Columbia Essays on Modern Writers Series: No. 41. New York: Columbia University Press, 1969.

Stevens, C. "Sound Systems of the Third Age of Middle-earth," *Quarterly Journal of Speech,* LIV (October 1968), 232–240.

Taylor, William L. "Frodo Lives: J.R.R. Tolkien's *The Lord of the Rings,*" *English Journal.* LVI (September 1967), 818–821.

Thomson, George M. *"The Lord of the Rings:* The Novel as Traditional Romance," *Wisconsin Studies in Contemporary Literature,* VIII (Winter 1967), 43–59.

Tinkler, John. "Old English in Rohan," pp. 164–169 in Isaacs and Zimbardo.

The Tolkien Papers. (Ten papers prepared for the Tolkien festival at Mankato State College, October 28–29, 1966,) *Mankato State College Studies,* II (February 1967).

Trowbridge, Clintown W. "The Twentieth Century British Supernatural Novel." Unpublished doctoral dissertation. Tallahassee, Florida: University of Florida, 1958.

Tyler, J.E. *The Tolkien Companion.* Illus. New York: St. Martin's Press, 1976.

West, Richard C. *Tolkien Criticism: An Annotated Checklist.* Kent, Ohio: Kent State University Press, 1970.

———. "Tolkien in the Letters of C.S. Lewis," *Orcrist #1,* 1966–67, pp. 2–16.

Wilson, Colin. "J.R.R. Tolkien," pp. 130–132 in the chapter "The Power of Darkness" in *The Strength to Dream: Literature and the Imagination.* London: Cambridge Press, 1962.

———. *Tree by Tolkien.* Santa Barbara, California: Capra Press, 1974.

Wojcik, Jan. "Tolkien and Coleridge: Remaking of the 'Green Earth'," *Renascence,* XX (Spring 1968). 134–139, 146.

Woods, Samuel, Jr. "J.R.R. Tolkien and the Hobbits," *Cimarron Review,* I (September 1962), 44–52.

Wright, Elizabeth. "Theology in the Novels of Charles Williams," *Stanford Honors Essays in Humanities,* 1962.

Wright, Marjorie Evelyn. "The Cosmic Kingdom of Myth: A Study in the Myth-Philosophy of Charles Williams, C. S. Lewis, and J.R.R. Tolkien." Unpublished doctoral dissertation. University of Illinois, 1960.

Zimbardo, Rose A. "Moral Vision in *The Lord of the Rings,*" pp. 100–108 in Isaacs and Zimbardo.

Solutions to Puzzles

THE HOBBIT: He was Gollum—as dark as darkness, except for two big round pale eyes in his thin face. He had a little boat, and he rowed about quite quietly on the lake; for lake it was, wide and deep and deadly cold. He paddled it with large feet dangling over the side, but never a ripple did he make. Not he.

WORDS:

- A. Thaumaturge
- B. Holiday
- C. Esgaroth
- D. Happened
- E. Old Tomnoddy
- F. Bullroarer
- G. Bedewed
- H. Ideal
- I. Tapped
- J. Oakenshield
- K. Requited
- L. The sword is sharp
- M. Hawhaw
- N. Edge of the wild
- O. Rivendell
- P. Excite
- Q. Arkenstone
- R. Nest
- S. Dead
- T. Beef
- U. Agitate
- V. Cut the cloth
- W. Kinsfolk
- X. Awake
- Y. Gandalf
- Z. Aquaplane
- Z1. Invisibility
- Z2. Needed

A 21 by 29 inch two-color print of the Arda map by Malcom Strandberg may be obtained by sending $5 to Arda Map, Box 15533, Sarasota, Florida 33579.

Acknowledgments

Thanks to all the people—too many, alas, to list by name—who responded to my letters and calls by helping to track down material for this book. The one person whose contribution could not have been more valuable was Frederick Patten. His enthusiasm, his access to elusive source materials, and his suggestions about discovering others, helped guide this book from an idea to a reality. I'm only sorry that I couldn't have followed up more of Fred's leads, which would have led, I suspect, to *The Tolkien Encyclopedia!*

Grateful acknowledgment is also made to the following publications and individuals for permission to reproduce materials:

"At the End of the Quest, Victory" by W. H. Auden originally appeared in the January 22, 1956 edition of *The New York Times Book Review.* Copyright © 1956 by The New York Times Company. Reprinted by permission.

"Oo, Those Awful Orcs" by Edmund Wilson appeared in *The Nation,* April 15, 1956. Copyright © 1956 The Nation Associates. Reprinted by permission.

"Tree by Tolkien" by Colin Wilson is adapted from a longer work of the same name. Copyright © 1974 Colin Wilson. Reprinted by permission of Capra Press.

"The Filial Duty of Christopher Tolkien" by William Cater originally appeared in the September 25, 1972, edition of *The Sunday Times Magazine,* London. Reprinted by permission.

"Two Views of J.R.R. Tolkien" by Kenneth Atchity originally appeared in the January 1978 issue of *The San Francisco Review of Books.* Reprinted by permission.

"The Evolution by Tolkien Fandom," an essay by Philip W. Helms, appeared in *Appendix T,* May 1977. Copyright © 1977 The American Tolkien Society.

"No Monroe in Lothlorien" by Arthur Weir originally appeared in *Triode* #17 and 18, January and May 1960. Reprinted by permission.

"Christmas at the South Pole" by J. R. Christopher. Appeared in *Minas Tirith Evening-Star: Journal of the American Tolkien Society,* vol. 6, no. 4, October 1976. Copyright © 1976 Philip and Marci Helms.

"A Baroque Memorial: J.R.R. Tolkien" by J.R. Christopher originally appeared in *Mythlore* 10. Copyright © 1975 The Mythopoeic Society, Inc. Reprinted by permission.

"The Picnic: A Parody of Tolkien" by Paulette Carroll originally appeared in *Orcrist,* vol. 1, no. 1. Reprinted by permission.

"The Coinage of Gondor and the Western Lands" by Dainis Bisieniks originally appeared in *Niekas* #16, June 30, 1966. Reprinted by permission.

"The Passing of the Elven-kind" by Ted Johnstone appeared in *Entmoot* #4, Spring 1967. Reprinted by permission.

"High Fly the Nazgul, Oh!" originally appeared in *I Palantir* #2, August 1961. Reprinted by permission.

"Middle-earth" and "Smaug the Magic Dragon" originally appeared in *The Middle-earth Songbook,* edited by Ruth Berman and Ken Nahigian. Reprinted by permission.

"The Orcs' Marching Song" by George Heap originally appeared in *Niekas* #8, March 15, 1964. Reprinted by permission.

"In the Service of the King," a short story by Marci Helms, appeared in *Minas Tirith Evening-Star: Journal of the American Tolkien Society,* vol. 5, no. 1, October 1975. Copyright © 1975 Philip and Marci Helms.

"Haiku Portraits" by Don Studebaker, Ted Johnstone, and others, originally appeared in *I Palantir* #2, August 1961, and *I Palantir* #3, April 1964. Reprinted by permission.

Arda Map copyright © 1978 Malcom B. Strandberg. Reprinted by permission.

Paintings copyright © 1974 Tim Kirk. Reprinted with permission of Rufus Publications, Inc.